FROM THE PECOS TO THE POWDER
A Cowboy's Autobiography

FROM THE
PECOS
TO THE
POWDER

A Cowboy's Autobiography

AS TOLD TO *Ramon F. Adams*

BY *Bob Kennon*

WITH DRAWINGS BY JOE BEELER
Foreword by Jimmy M. Skaggs

UNIVERSITY OF OKLAHOMA PRESS
NORMAN AND LONDON

DEDICATED

to the memory of Charlie Russell and all the other old-time cowmen of Montana who knew him so well.

LIBRARY OF CONGRESS CATALOG CARD NUMBER: 65–10113
ISBN: 0–8061–2212–9

TABLE OF CONTENTS

Maps

FOREWORD

By Jimmy M. Skaggs

AS HE RELATES in the Preface, Ramon F. Adams—self-taught folklorist, foremost lay historian of the range-cattle era, and highly respected critical bibliographer of the American West—was approached at mid-century by Florence Franklin, a stranger, who told him about octogenarian Montana rancher Bob Kennon, her brother-in-law. He had been a close friend of Western artist Charles M. Russell, whose biography Adams and Homer E. Britzman had published in 1948, and she encouraged Adams to "write [Kennon's] story."

Eventually Adams contacted the cattleman and discovered that, despite his age, his mind was still sharp and clear. In fact, the old man was soon sending Adams "more material . . . than [he] could use." *From the Pecos to the Powder, a cowboy's autobiography*, by Bob Kennon as told to Ramon F. Adams, was the result.

Published in 1965 by the University of Oklahoma Press, the book received mixed reviews but was generally judged a worthy addition to the body of knowledge about that most colorful institution of the American West, the range-cattle industry.[1]

Reared in Texas, during his youth Kennon had trekked from ranch to ranch as drover and cowhand, eventually working from Mexico to the Canadian border before finally settling down in

[1]For examples, see West Texas Historical Association *Year book*, 41 (1965), p. 179; *Saturday review* 48 (May 22, 1965), p. 84; *Library journal* 90 (March 15, 1965), p. 1313; *Journal of American history*, 52 (March 1965), p. 840.

ix

Montana. His reminiscences of the vanishing frontier entwines with wild frontier towns, skinflint ranchers, irascible camp cooks, cowboy artist "Charlie" Russell, and much, much more.

About each Kennon offered revealing observations and, frequently, amusing anecdotes. He cowboyed in west Texas and, in his own words, "grew up over night" in El Paso, where "they killed over cards, women, horses, or just plain orneryness. . . ." When he and a friend tried to hire on with a miserly west Texas stockman, the old man led them to believe they were on the payroll, fed them, then charged them for their meals —"the worst insult a person could receive. . . ." The cowboys found an original way to get even. Interesting characters include a cook with a weak stomach, a French chef who encounters a rattlesnake, and a particularly fastidious cook called "Dirty Dave." Especially valuable are Kennon's recollections of his friend Charlie Russell, through whose paintings much of the color of the American West was preserved. Perhaps the book's best tale relates to a mail-order bride who mistook Russell for her intended.

Kennon's varied life also included stints as forest ranger, stock inspector, deputy sheriff, and doorkeeper for the Montana Senate, each of which provide entertaining yarns for the book. Now, a quarter century after its publication, it is still a good read, largely because of Ramon Adams's talent as a storyteller.

Born on October 3, 1889, in Moscow (Polk County), Texas, to Cooke M. and Charlie (Colby) Adams, Ramon Frederick Adams grew up near Houston; in Peoria, Illinois; and in Sherman, Texas, where his father was a jeweler. He attended Captain John H. LeTellier's private school for boys in Sherman and entered Austin College as a sub-freshman at age sixteen. Within two years he was editing *Reveille*, a monthly student magazine, but in 1909, before completing his sophomore year, he withdrew to study violin with Carl Venth, a noted teacher at Sherman's Kidd-Key Conservatory of Music.

In 1912, Adams joined the faculty of the music department at the University of Arkansas, where he taught violin for two years. While in Fayetteville he met, courted, and married Allie Jarman. Afterward, he studied and taught briefly in Chicago before returning to Texas in 1916 to head the violin department at Wichita Falls College of Music, supplementing his income by conducting an orchestra at the local Majestic Theatre. The Rialto in Fort Worth soon lured him away with more money, and he played violin in its pit until 1923, when a musicians' strike left him unemployed. Moving to Dallas, he found work at the Palace Theater and with the Symphony Orchestra, but his music career ended abruptly in 1929 when he broke his wrist cranking his Model T Ford.

He had a son, Elman, to rear and to support, and at his wife's encouragement, he purchased a candy store in downtown Dallas. For more than a quarter century they operated it as the Adams Candy Company, which became a popular gathering place for Dallasites. In addition to a prosperous retail trade, the Adamses soon developed a successful wholesale business, furnishing such delicacies as Burnt Offering and Texas Pe-Candy to area retailers, including Neiman-Marcus. In 1956 the Adamses sold the business and retired.

By then Ramon F. Adams was a leading authority on the nineteenth-century trans-Mississippi West. He had commenced his scholarly literary career while still a musician, privately publishing his first book in Vancouver in 1919: *Poems of the Canadian west.* He did not sell his first article until 1923, when *Western story magazine* bought a piece about cowboys.[2] Then, during the 1930s, he began to write seriously. "I'd close the store at 11 P.M., then come

---

[2]Gerald D. Saxon, "Ramon Adams collection register" (MS, 1986, Dallas Public Library), p. 1; Edward Hake Phillips, "A sketch of Ramon F. Adams" (MS, 1987, Archives, Austin College, Sherman, Texas), p. 1. See also *National union catalog* (Washington: Library of Congress, various issues).

home and spend several hours writing at the old kitchen table," he later recalled. "It was a hard way to write a book."[3]

He wrote primarily about what he knew best, what interested him most—American cowboys. As a child on the outskirts of Houston he had made friends with the men who drove cattle along a nearby trail and who frequently stopped off for a meal with the Adamses. He was enthralled by their vivid tales and earthy language, a fascination that remained with him for life. He pursued the topic diligently in his spare time, eventually traveling across the United States conducting research and collecting material.

The first product of that labor was *Cowboy lingo* (Boston: Houghton Mifflin Co., 1936), a book J. Frank Dobie considered indispensable to understanding life on the range.[4] It was followed by *Western words; a dictionary of the range, cow camp, and trail* (Norman: University of Oklahoma Press, 1944; 2d ed., 1968, issued under the revised subtitle *A dictionary of the American West*); with H. E. Britzman, *Charles M. Russell, the cowboy artist* (Pasadena, Calif.: Trail's End Pub. Co., 1948; 2d ed., 1954; 3d ed., 1957); *Come an' get it; the story of the old cowboy cook* (Oklahoma, 1952); *The legendary West* (Dallas: Friends of the Dallas Library, 1965); *Six-guns and saddle leather; a bibliography of books and pamphlets on western outlaws and gunmen* (Oklahoma, 1954; 2d ed., 1969); *The best of the American cowboy* (Oklahoma, 1957; translated by Luciano Bianciardi and published in Milano by Feltrinelli, 1958; *The rampaging herd; a bibliography of books and pamphlets on men and events in the cattle industry* (Oklahoma, 1959); *A fitting death for Billy the kid* (Oklahoma, 1960); *Old time cowhand* (New York: Macmillan, 1961); and *Burs under the saddle; a second look at books and histories of the West* (Oklahoma, 1964), followed by *From the Pecos to the Pow-*

---

[3] Ramon F. Adams, *Old-time cowhand* (New York: Macmillan, 1961) [dust jacket].

[4] J. Frank Dobie, *Life and literature of the Southwest; revised and enlarged in both knowledge and wisdom* (Dallas: Southern Methodist University Press, 1952), p. 95.

der (1965).

Then came *The cowman & his philosophy* (Austin: Encino Press, 1967); *The cowboy and his humor* (Encino, 1968); *The cowman & his code of ethics* (Encino, 1969); *Wayne Gard, historian of the West* (Austin: Steck-Vaughn Co., 1970); *The cowman says it salty* (Tucson: University of Arizona Press, 1971); *The horse wrangler & his remuda* (Encino, 1971); a compilation, *The Adams one-fifty; a checklist of the 150 most important books on Western outlaws* (Austin: Jenkins Co., 1976); *The language of the railroader* (Oklahoma, 1977); and *More burs under the saddle; books and histories of the West* (Oklahoma, 1979).[5] At the time of his death, on April 29, 1976, at age 86, Adams was gathering material on John R. Bouldin—cowboy, Arizona pioneer, and writer—about whom he planned to pen a biography.[6]

Unlike many if not most western writers, Adams's works have appealed to both scholars and buffs, leading his friend and fellow lay historian Wayne Gard to contend that, "Except for O. Henry, Walter Prescott Webb, and J. Frank Dobie, [Adams] is the most quoted Texas author ever. . . . He is known and quoted wherever the English language is spoken."[7]

Surely that fact was not lost on Savoie Lottinville, director of the University of Oklahoma Press, who understood his market. When *From the Pecos to the Powder* was published, he ordered that Adams's name alone should appear on the book's spine. Cowboy Bob Kennon was almost totally lost in his editor's shadow.

[5]Several of these titles have been reprinted by other publishers, such as *Old-time cowhand* (New York: Collier Books, 1971) and *Rampaging herd* (Beverly Hills, Calif.: International Bookfinders, [c1977]).

[6]See Ramon Adams Collection, Register MA82–6, Dallas, Texas, Public Library.

[7]Quoted in Karen Klinefelter, "Folklorist enjoys 3rd career; ex-violinist and candy merchant writes about old West," *Dallas Morning-News*, October 26, 1969, p. 38A. For a more disparaging view of Adams (and, for that matter, of most historians of the range-cattle era), see Don D. Walker, *Clio's cowboys; studies in the historiography of the cattle trade* (Lincoln: University of Nebraska Press, 1981), pp. xi, xvi, 4, 46, 77–78.

I FIRST became interested in Bob Kennon when I learned he was a close friend of Charlie Russell. His sister-in-law, Mrs. Florence Franklin, had read my book *Charles M. Russell, the Cowboy Artist* and had written me that Mr. Kennon was a great friend of the artist. She also told me that he had led an interesting life and asked if I would write his story. She gave me some material, and we corresponded for some time before I began writing Mr. Kennon direct.

Although in his eighties, Mr. Kennon began sending me the story of his life—more material, in fact, than I could use. He had a keen memory and a deep interest in the history of his state. A typical cowboy, he did not marry until late in life because of his love for the freedom of his profession: that right to wander as he pleased, see new country, and make new friends. He never seemed quite ready to settle down. For many years he bore an outstanding reputation as a bronc rider, getting his nickname, "Kickin' Bob," from the expert way in which he "kicked out" these bad horses.

When his cowboy days were nearly over, he took a wife and held such responsible jobs as forest ranger, stock inspector, deputy sheriff, and doorkeeper for the state senate, besides being a rancher himself. He was well known throughout Montana and could count his friends by the number of his acquaintances. Although the Kennons never had children of their own, their home was a gathering place for young people, and many hours of pleasure were spent at this mecca of fun for both young and old.

I think every pioneer Westerner has a story to tell, and failure to tell it means that much Western history is lost. Mr. Kennon, for example, relates some anecdotes about Charlie Russell which have never been in print before, and there are tales about his own life, observations on customs of the country, and descriptions of Montana which would never have come to light had he not jotted them down for another generation to read.

The reader may object to the mention of so much drinking or to the many references to saloons, but in those days it was a way of life for the cowman. There were very few cowboys who did not drink to some extent when they hit town; it was their mode of being sociable and their relaxation. And let me say here and now that the Western saloon was not the den of iniquity the pious would have it be. It was an important establishment and filled a need in a womanless country. It was, in fact, about the only place where a man could loaf and be welcome; where he could meet friends, warm himself in winter, secure a job for the following spring or fall, and make new friends—and sometimes enemies. The average cowhand did no drinking until he went to town; hence it is not surprising that he indulged himself when he did get with friends, who, like himself, had been through a long drought. So if you think Mr. Kennon refers to drinking unduly, just remember, it was the custom of the country during his day and no one was thought any the less of for this indulgence.

It is my hope that this book will give you a picture of life in the early days of Montana's cattle industry, as well as a few hours of relaxation, and that when you finish reading it, you will feel as well acquainted with Mr. Kennon as I do.

DALLAS, TEXAS   *Ramon F. Adams*

JANUARY 1, 1965

xvi

FROM THE PECOS TO THE POWDER

A Cowboy's Autobiography

CHAPTER I

In Retrospect

PERHAPS I am the last living rider of those boys who, in 1896, came up that long trail to Montana from what was then the largest ranch in the world, the Terrazas Ranch in Old Mexico. At least I know of none of the boys still living, for in the years that have passed we have become separated like the trail dust we made, and have lived our lives far from one another.

After arriving in Montana we lingered around Old Milestown for a time, finding jobs punching cows and breaking broncs. But it was not long until we eagerly sought new worlds to conquer, for we were young, full of life and fun, and our days and nights never seemed long enough to live life to the full.

We had come from all the way from beyond the Mexican border to Montana with a big herd belonging to two famous men —Mr. Broadus and Mr. Hysham. Our trail boss was Mr. Baker. Today, three cities of eastern Montana still bear their names: Broadus, Hysham, and Baker. These men had brought up many herds from Texas, but this time they had come into Mexico to buy cattle from Don Luis Terrazas where I was working.

Though this happened a very long time ago, it seems but yesterday. I sometimes think the whiter a man's hair becomes, the greener grow his memories. During these intervening years I've met hundreds of people from Mexico to the Canadian border, punched cows and broken broncs for most of the big and famous outfits of Montana, and I wouldn't trade these memories for all the world's goods.

As I look back upon my life, it seems to me that time is divided into four portions, which, like the day, begin with the dawn, run high to noon, lengthen into sunset, then darken into night. I'm now in my sunset years, and before night falls, I feel that I must

tell this story. In it are the stories of the boys with whom I rode and worked. Together we shared all the experiences on the cattle range and in the gold-mining camps of the day. Of course many of the little towns where so much happened to us were only stage stations, often only a barn where the relay teams were changed. Blacksmith shops were necessary and of course a saloon, sometimes a "hotel," and a store handling general supplies, often with a tiny post office in one corner.

Montana at this time was a vast cattle empire, though many big sheep outfits came in later. The people were a hospitable lot of openhearted folks, welcoming all creeds and classes at their firesides. It was then a man's country, composed of cowmen, sheepmen, saloonkeepers, stage drivers, gamblers, Chinese cafe owners, drifters, and saddle tramps. Occasionally we came across a Catholic priest performing his lonely duty among the Indians and in the hellhole of the mining camps. Sometimes, too, a Protestant sky-pilot would share our camp or find rest at some friendly ranch.

The land itself was magnificent with its untamed beauty of grassy plains and valleys, its mountains of hazy blue and purple. These mountains were always visible, for it seemed that wherever we rode, they were there, often near, sometimes far away. Montana is still called the Land of the Shining Mountains.

In the fall of the year the beef herds fattened on the tall, golden grass, were then rounded up and driven to the nearest shipping point. They were driven slowly so that they would not lose the weight and the bloom they had taken on during the spring and summer months.

Many thousands of sheep were also shipped to market. Lonely sheepherders tended these "woolies," making their home in a camp wagon. Sometimes they had no one to talk to for months, except the faithful dog, usually an Australian shepherd, which helped these herders tend their big bands.

All this was before the sod-busters and homesteaders came in. The stockman's domain was really an unfenced and wonderful world, unlike anything we know today. No wonder the changes of civilization sickened Charlie Russell and made his artistic soul resentful. It was he who said: "History and romance died when the plow turned the country grass side down."

The things which cannot change are the matchless sunsets and the glory of the sunrises. There the sun may be seen painting its way across the new day. Early risers on a summer morning can behold it, even as riders did in the old range days. Many places are still unspoiled by man, among which are the rugged river brakes along the Missouri, the Musselshell, and the Yellowstone. But gone forever are the herds of antelope, deer, and elk, though there are reserves for wild animals and hunting in season is permitted today. Perhaps you can picture Montana when the big herds came up the long trail to Milestown. That is my hope, my purpose now.

For my humble beginnings I'll take you back to Texas, where I was born and where I spent my childhood. When I returned to my Texas home many years later, things looked different and many changes had taken place since my boyhood. My dad's old horse ranch on the Sweetwater was just a landmark. It had the same sky over it, the same hills, creeks, and trees, but the trees had grown tall, with mighty spreading branches. It didn't seem that I'd been gone so long until I looked at those old trees. There they stood, so grand, representing my lost years, during which my family had become scattered.

I remember the great fun we kids used to have in those trees, for they were big even when I was still a boy. We used to climb high in the branches and hang like monkeys. Unless it was terribly hot, we always went barefooted and bareheaded, but if we did wear caps or hats, it was a game to throw each other's headgear up among the branches.

When I looked up into one of those trees, I saw some horseshoes I had thrown up over a branch for a stunt. The limb had grown over them, and it made a pretty sight to me. I wanted them sawed out so that I could take them back to Montana with me,

7

and the owner, a very nice fellow, obliged me. He presented them to me when I left that evening.

I took this piece home in my trunk and kept it for years, using it for a fancy doorstop at the ranch. I liked having it where I could see it, but in moving my ranch business around, I became afraid it would get lost, so I gave it to the Cowboys' Museum at Great Falls for safekeeping. This museum, at the Fair Grounds, is full of old reminders of the cattle days. I have loaned it quite a collection of things, such as old brand books, my Mexican sombrero and spurs, my fancy pearl and silver gun with my name engraved upon its stock. I have often thumbed through these old brand books, picturing the very critters which carried those brands. I often recall the outfits for which I rode, and see that long, long trail at the beginning of the time I was a kid on my dad's horse ranch in Texas.

Yes, I guess I can remember all these things far better than I can those things which happened just a few years back. I wish I could ride again in the old Red Bird stagecoach that I loaned to Old Town there on the Fair Grounds. It would beat, bumps and all, any trip in a Pullman, for the days of stagecoaches, cattle, and horses were days that meant something, and the folks were *real*, be they good or bad.

What a man I thought I was, too, when I started out from the Sweetwater country and tried to make it alone. In those days nothing in the world ever licked us young fellows. After my dad tried ranching in the country around Merkel, he moved to a ranch on the Sweetwater. Here he raised horses and for once seemed to be contented.

Kids those days were raised in the saddle. I was riding alone when most kids were being told fairy tales. But the kids I knew grew up independent-like, and we were out with the men. We had so much to keep us happy and out of doors all day. We watched all the branding of colts and cattle, the shoeing of horses, and believe me, some of those horses were mighty hard to shoe.

Mother died when I was just a little shaver, and after that I ran wild with the older kids as we roamed over the prairies. We learned fast that we had to stick or get left behind. We had races which took us far from home. In this way we missed a lot of meals and got some switchings to make us stay closer to home, for it was dangerous to get lost or be afoot in those days where there were a lot of animals that were killers.

Texas has a sort of scent and fragrance in my memory. Its pine and cactus and yucca, the sweetness of the wild flowers—all these bring back memories. We were forever fetching home big bouquets of these flowers to my ailing mother, for she loved them. There were bluebonnets, the Indian paintbrush, the Indian blanket, primroses, daisies, and wild phlox.

I can think of hundreds of plants and some pests, too, like the loco weed. The milkweed, too, was a pest, though I knew Mexicans who claimed the white blossoms a sure cure for ringworm and snake bite. I remember how it was around San Angelo when I rode that country in the spring or early summer. The patches of flowers were like a quilt worked out in yellow, blue, orange-red, pink, and purple. That had been buffalo country. When the folks I knew were young and started ranches, they claim to have been obliged to chase herds of buffalo away from their holdings. The bones told the truth of this story.

I'd love to hear a mockingbird, too. Unless you come from the South, you'd never believe how sweet they sing and how they can imitate. There were bobwhites and pretty little doves; all were good company to a kid out alone.

When I think of the wild game we used to have when I was a boy, I feel cheated for growing up. We had prairie chickens, grouse, and pheasants and all such birds. Those were the days! The streams were full of fish, and we had venison. You know of the black-tailed Mexican deer and the white-tail. I've heard that there are no more of the pronghorn antelope or the Texas big-horn sheep. I guess, though, they have some of the wild turkeys left, and these were sure swell eating when young.

In a way it was a paradise, though dangerous if kids were left out alone. We were fearful of snakes, for they were of tremen-dous size, sometimes eight or ten feet in length, and there were diamondback rattlers, and cottonmouths near the water. Often we heard of someone killing a coral snake, and farther east were the deadly copperheads.

A kid could hunt, fish, and trap. The best fur-bearing animals were the red and gray foxes, the beaver, and the muskrat. There were all kinds of squirrels and rabbits, to say nothing of badgers and, of course, skunks, if you wanted to get into trouble at home. We had a very painful and fragrant memory of Mr. Skunk and were cured.

But I was growing up, and what started me out on my own was the fact that my dad got married to a widow with a houseful of kids of her own. Not that she wasn't a good woman, but somehow I felt it was my time to leave. Secretly I was tickled to death to have such a good excuse for leaving home. I hated to hurt my father, but after the trouble I had with my stepbrothers when Father was away, I knew the only answer for me was to leave home. But first I must start at the very beginning, so that you will really understand how all these things came to be.

CHAPTER II

My Early Years

I WAS BORN in Cedar Hill, Texas, eighteen miles southwest of Dallas, on the eighth of September, 1876. My father was Captain Ad P. Kennon, a soldier in the Civil War and a Texas pioneer. He was born in Dublin, Ireland, and came to this country when a small boy to live with his brothers, who had emigrated to America from Ireland several years earlier. They had settled near Shreveport, Louisiana, where they acquired a cotton plantation.

My mother's name was Stella Mitchell, and her birthplace was Nashville, Tennessee. Her father was born in Glasgow, Scotland, and he was a scholarly, educated gentleman. Coming to this country, he settled at Nashville, where he became president of the First Baptist College of Nashville. Grandmother Mitchell was a fullblooded Spanish woman, born and reared in Madrid, Spain. Her parents sent her to America to study at the college at Nashville. While at college she met and married Grandad Mitchell. Only one child was born to this union, a daughter Stella, my mother. She grew to womanhood in Nashville, attended school there, and later received her higher education at the Baptist College. All this happened before the Civil War.

Dad was a handsome young fellow. When he left Shreveport to visit friends in Nashville, he met Mother at a party given by friends of Mother's family. They fell in love, and after a whirlwind courtship, married in Nashville.

Following their marriage, Dad took his young bride back to the plantation at Shreveport, to the family home of his people. Shortly after their marriage, war clouds began to gather. Dad enlisted with the Confederate forces at the very start of the war, served the full duration, and was discharged with the rank of captain at the war's end.

During the years of the war, Mother continued to make the plantation her home. In this period of time she had given birth to a son. Among the many plantation slaves was a kindly old darky who was most devoted to my young mother.

"What shall I name this little boy?" Mother asked him one day.

"Call him Judge, for that's one of the greatest names anywhere," replied this old man.

So Mother did as he asked and my brother was named Judge.

When Father returned to the plantation at the close of the war, Judge was almost four years old. Father remained home for six years, but the old Southern home was not the happy place it had been. After three of my sisters, Sally, Nancy, and Allie, were born on the old plantation, our parents decided to take their family and go overland by ox team to that great empire, with its vast plains and rivers, known as Texas. These young people had the will to make a new home in a new land, also the high courage and determination to work and succeed. They settled near Cedar Hill, Texas, established a home, and entered the cattle business. At Cedar Hill my sisters Addie and Ida, my brother Willie, and myself were born. Willie died in his childhood while we lived there.

We loved our home dearly. Texas was a land of vast expanses, free land, countless ways to make money in the livestock game, so our herd continued to expand. Dad also dealt in mules, buying and selling at a profit. St. Louis was the leading mule market. The Wallensteins, mule buyers of that city, came down and bought our mules. We trailed them into Dallas, a trip of eighteen miles. This was Judge's job and one he loved because he liked to ride. He was now about eighteen years of age. He rode a saddle horse and led an old white bell mare, which the mules would follow. Dad owned half-interest in the feed yard in Dallas on the banks of the Trinity River, and to this yard Judge took the mules to be delivered to the mule buyers. Dad also dealt in cotton, buying up bales from the surrounding cotton farmers. Cotton buyers would come to the auction held at the ranch and buy the cotton.

My years at Cedar Hill were those before I reached school age, and so most of my memories here are of the pranks we played and the various incidents in the lives of us children. We kept calves in a corral near the house. Sister Ida and I had a small saddle, and we would put this on the top pole of the corral and imagine we were on horses. When we got tired of playing, we'd forget to take the saddle down, or, as children do, didn't think it necessary. One night Dad heard a noise at the corral. He always kept his double-barreled shotgun loaded and was a great hand to swear. He let out some fancy cuss words and yelled, "Speak up! Who are you?" There was no answer. In the darkness he mistook the saddle for a man, and he cut loose with a blast from the shotgun and riddled our little saddle.

We had two bulldogs named Bull and Watch. These fellows had a deep fear of thunder and lightning. When a thunderstorm developed, they always came into the house and crawled under the bed. I, too, was under the bed one time having a fill of brown sugar, not having candy in abundance as children do today. My sisters had taken me to school on this particular day, and not liking school, I ran home and crawled under the bed. When Mother found me, I was under there with the bulldogs and they were busy licking brown sugar from my face.

Dad had an old-fashioned rocking chair, a homemade affair

with long rockers. It had a cowhide seat and back and there was an arrangement in front upon which he could place his feet and rest them while he read. On this particular occasion he was deeply interested in his newspaper. The temptation was just too much, so I tied a rawhide string on old Bull's collar, got him up close to the rocker, and said, "Sic 'em!" Poor Dad, the chair went out from under him and his head hit the floor so hard that for a moment or two he was speechless. I beat it away from there for I knew I was in for a thrashing, but he soon caught me and I got a good one.

Mother kept a flock of geese for the feathers she used to make her feather beds and pillows. An old goose hen was setting under the porch, and an old gander was always there guarding her. Allie said she would crawl under the porch to see if any young ones had hatched. In those days striped bed ticking was the material used for dresses, and Allie was attired in one of these creations with nothing under the dress but skin. The old gander nabbed her, and she let out an awful shriek, but the old gander held on until she pulled him out from under the porch.

Not many years ago Allie was a saleslady in the dress and sportswear department of Neiman-Marcus in Dallas. Seeing her well groomed and a polished lady, I couldn't help but grin when I thought of her in the dresses of her childhood.

One of my bad habits was running away and hiding in the corn field near the house, so my sisters decided to break me of this stunt. They mixed up some dough, smeared it on their faces as masks, leaving holes for mouth and eyes, donned white sheets, and went out as prowling ghosts to scare me home. This they succeeded in doing, and I beat them both home, for I wasn't too sure they weren't real ghosts.

While we lived at Cedar Hill, a peddler came around regularly. He bought almost anything you could name—eggs, butter, chickens, hides, sheep pelts. He had a spring wagon with the seat built up high so he could drive his team without difficulty. On this particular day he stopped in Cedar Hill to inquire where he could buy more produce. He had a large coop covered with chicken wire so he could keep all the poultry inside. As he started out of Cedar Hill, two boys unfastened the latch on the chicken coop, and all the chickens flew out. Poor man, he was so intent on driving down the road that he was unaware of this prank until he reached Duncanville, about eight miles from Cedar Hill. He certainly lost money on that chicken deal.

We lived in an old house at Cedar Hill many years before Dad built a new one, a two-story home with a veranda all around, both up- and downstairs. This house was thirty by sixty feet, with four large bedrooms upstairs, hallway and stairs right in the center of the downstairs. There was a parlor, as front rooms were then called, entrance hall, dining room, two downstairs bedrooms, kitchen, and bath. Upstairs had a screened porch, and there was a full basement walled up with cedar logs. There was a deep well under the back porch where Judge always watered his race mare from a cedar bucket. He used to warn me not to tell Mother that he used this bucket to water his horse.

Mother's health was beginning to fail, so our family doctor, Dr. Roberts, advised Dad to locate in a higher, drier climate, where he thought she might be better. Dad took a trip to Abilene, Texas, to look at a cow ranch. He bought 640 acres southwest of Trent, just four miles from town. He then returned to Cedar Hill and sold the old ranch to some people from Dallas. Leaving the old home was a sad but exciting adventure for us kids.

Trent was on the Texas and Pacific Railroad. Judge was a grown man by now and was of great assistance to Dad in the cow business. Before they could take all the horses and cattle to this new location, it was necessary to fence at least a portion of the land. So Dad leased a large pasture near Cedar Hill, seven or eight miles west, and Judge and Henry Tanner held the stock there until they could trail them overland to Trent. Mother, my grown sisters, and we small ones stayed at Cedar Hill until Dad had the house built and the furniture in readiness for our arrival.

Dad fenced the land, dug a well, hauled timber from Abilene, a distance of thirty-five miles, secured the help of carpenters, and built a square house facing east. It had a lean-to on each side and a front and back porch. There was lots of mesquite in this country, and they had to grub some of this off before they could build the house.

Dad had completed the house and accomplished many other things before he came by train to Cedar Hill and took the family to the new home in West Texas. Judge and several other young Texans—Al Cornelius, who later married my sister Nancy; Henry Tanner, who later was chief of police in Dallas for years; Sam Treese, who had married my older sister Sally several years previously—trailed the cattle and horses overland. They had a wagon loaded with supplies and bedding. These boys took turns driving the wagon. After a hard trip of several weeks, they pulled in at the ranch. Dad had men clear up about fifty acres of mesquite, plowed this with oxen, and planted maize, kafir corn, and corn for winter feed.

By now I'd reached school age, and along with my older sisters, we walked four miles to a primitive log schoolhouse. The construction of this little seat of learning deserves some mention. There was a trench dug all the way around, about eighteen by twenty feet square; the logs were set straight up and down in this trench and reached about seven feet high. They were covered with poles, brush, and dirt to make a roof, and the floor was of dirt. Poles were placed against the upright logs to hold them steady, about three poles to the side. These poles were wrapped with rawhide to hold them in place. Windows and doors were cut, and a square of rawhide the size of the door or window was nailed to a thin pole. This was passed along the door or window, pulled open or shut according to the needs of the weather. The logs were chinked with mud and grass to help keep out the weather.

The desks were long, hand hewn from rough lumber brought from Abilene. We sat on long benches. An aisle divided the room, and the boys sat on one side, the girls on the other. We had no blackboard and there were no slates. It was the third year before we got those luxuries. Later they built a better building, using this first schoolhouse as a horse barn.

About a mile from the schoolhouse was a small creek. At noon we boys would go over there for a swim, or rather to wade around. On one occasion the girls slipped over to the swimming hole and stole our clothes. The boys took after them and reclaimed their clothes, but being the smallest, I didn't get mine back. I went into the schoolroom crying and without clothes. The teacher made me go back outside and find my clothes. Even today I surely would love to get even with those girls.

CHAPTER III

Boyish Pranks

MOTHER'S HEALTH continued to fail, and Dad bought a new home in Merkel so she could be near a doctor and have medical attention. We had lived in Merkel something over a year when she died. Three of my sisters had now married, thus leaving Dad with us younger ones.

After about a year, Dad married again, taking for his wife a widow with five children of her own. The home in Merkel was now sold, and Dad's new family, my little sisters, and myself returned to the Trent ranch to make our home. Of my stepmother's children, three were grown and married; the remaining two were small boys.

My stepmother was a religious woman and a member of the Christian Church. The church's communion wine was always kept at our house in her care, stored in gallon jugs. One Sunday morning she and Dad, with the smallest son, left for church in the buggy, instructing us boys to follow on horseback. The son they left behind was about three years older than I, and when they left for church, he went into the house and got a jug of wine. He took a drink and told me to take one. West of the house, about two or three hundred yards, was a heavy growth of mesquite. We went into this and continued to drink. After a few drinks we began to fight, and then we got sick.

The way our parents trailed us was by the vomit we left behind. When finally found, we were widely separated, for we had wandered apart. My stepmother was both shocked and angry.

They took us home and put us to bed. The next morning, she and Dad had a quarrel, for she blamed me, and when Dad left for town, she warmed me over good with a rawhide quirt.

Another job she always laid out for me was carrying wash water a distance of a quarter-mile in two cedar buckets. Because I was always sorefooted, this was quite a task for me. I had to fill a big iron kettle with this water, and she heated it for the washing. I remember being envious of my brother Judge at this time because he decided to leave home. He went north to Montana, where he secured employment as a cowhand with the cattle firm of Milner and Bodman, whose ranch was located on Shonkin Creek in the Fort Benton area in what is now Chouteau County.

Mr. Milner, a close friend of Buffalo Bill Cody, had a beautiful ranch home which in those days was considered a mansion. A tree-lined driveway with countless birdhouses first attracted one's attention. Each tree had been named for some cowboy employed by the ranch. There were beautiful flower gardens, one strictly for roses, and in the back yard there was an artesian well with a quaint well house.

This home was fully staffed with efficient servants, and Buffalo Bill was often a guest. Sad to relate, at Mr. Milner's death this fine property was sold to other interests and was soon in a sad state of disrepair. Today some of the beautiful trees remain and some of the birdhouses may yet be seen, but few remember the proud past of this estate.

One time when Buffalo Bill was a guest of Milner, he persuaded Judge to join his Wild West Show. My brother was known as Black Bear because of his dark, swarthy coloring. The Wild West Show toured Continental Europe, the British Isles, and the United States. Judge loved the thrill and excitement of the show world, with its marvelous chance for travel in foreign lands. At the termination of the tour, Judge came back to Texas. Here he made his home with his sister and brother-in-law, Sam

Treese, who owned a ranch near Trent, just a mile from our old ranch home, which Dad had now sold.

It wasn't long until Dad and his new wife began to quarrel over us kids, and they separated. Dad took us children back to our old home in Merkel. Sam Treese and Judge were operating the Treese Ranch at Trent, running both cattle and horses. Judge always had a keen love for good horses and had about two hundred head of them. He continued riding as much as his health would allow. He had previously suffered a back injury while riding for Buffalo Bill, and it was while he was helping to run one of Father's horse ranches near Trent that he received a fatal injury. One morning he went out to wrangle the saddle horses, and while he was riding at a fast lope, his horse stepped into a badger hole and fell on top of him, breaking his back. I had gone to a grocery store in Merkel to get some groceries and was returning home when Sister Addie came running to meet me. "Judge has been hurt," she cried.

After Judge's death, Sam Treese and his family decided to move back to Cedar Hill. Before their return, Dad, my little sisters, and myself lived with them for a time. When they moved back, Dad took my sisters to Abilene, where he bought a home, and while they lived there, I went to make my home with Grandma Treese. She was a typical Texas ranch woman. I lived with her for several months and liked it because life there was interesting and exciting. She wore those wide-skirted dresses with long sleeves down to the back of her hand, wore her hair in two long braids, beautiful black hair wrapped around her head like a coronet. All her children were grown and married and she enjoyed having me for company.

It was my job to go and get the milch cows from the pasture. The nettles were very bad, and since I went barefooted, she would wrap cloth around my legs to keep the nettles from stinging. The old cows were in a pasture up the creek about half a mile

Bob Kennon riding his horse Concho. He was repping for the 79 when this photograph was made.

Cowboys rounding up cattle for the 79 near Miles City, Montana.

north of the house. I was taking my time about getting them, when I came upon a huge swarm of flies and smelled a dreadful odor. Looking up, I saw a Negro hanging by the neck from a big pecan tree, his tongue sticking out. I was so scared I ran all the way back to the house and told Grandma what I'd seen.

"Take me to this place and we'll see what this is all about," she said.

"I don't want to go back there," I said as I cried.

But she insisted that I take her, so we both took off down the path, she holding me by the hand, I keeping behind her, for she knew I'd bolt if she turned me loose. I was holding Grandma's wide skirt out with one hand so I wouldn't see the gruesome sight. We came to the spot at last, and when she let loose my hand, I ran back to the house as fast as my legs would carry me. Coming back to the house, Grandma hooked up a team to the buckboard and took me along with her to Duncanville, where she reported this incident to the sheriff. It was learned this Negro had raped a white girl, and some white men had stretched his neck.

One of Grandma's sons thought it would be a fine gift if he would give her a brand-new cookstove. Then she would no longer need to cook in the fireplace. They brought the stove to her ranch and put it up, but she refused to cook or bake on this newfangled thing. She made her pies, cakes, and wonderful biscuits in her fireplace. I never saw any light bread until I came north, nor yellow corn meal. Southern people always used white corn meal.

When I went to visit Grandma, I had a pet prairie dog which she said I might bring along, but she wasn't familiar with the ways of these little animals of West Texas. When we arrived at her home, I turned Mr. Prairie Dog loose, but not for long, for he cut down all her fine rosebushes and dug holes in her yard. This was just too much, and she took her old shotgun and riddled him.

There was a big spring west of her house with a log spring house over it. The water was very cold and wonderful to drink as it bubbled from solid rock. Here is where she kept her milk and butter, nor was there ever a better deepfreeze.

She also had a two-acre orchard of peaches and other fruit, and a herd of bee gums, where the bees stored their honey. These bee gums were made of hewn trees. They would take a big cedar or elm tree and saw it down. They then sawed this up in board lengths and made the bee gums out of these, using wooden pins, as they had no nails. They made squares inside with sticks, much as beehives are made today, for the bees to store their honey. Holes were bored underneath the gum so that the bees could go in and out. These bee gums were set up on stumps in order to be off the ground. When the bees began to swarm, we would ring bells, beat on cans, or pour water, and the bees would settle on a tree limb or some other place. Then we would brush the bees off and put them in these bee gums. Thus we always had bees and plenty of honey.

Grandma had a pet antelope she kept picketed on a forty-foot rawhide rope which I helped her make. When making the rope, we put the hide in a bowl of wood ashes and water so as to take off all the hair. After we stretched it as tight as we could, we left it for several days. We then made an apparatus from two sticks: bored a hole in the first one, put the other through the bored hole and fastened it in place with a wooden pin. One of these sticks held the end of the hide, the other one turned the hide, and thus we twisted the hide into a rope. I've often made rawhide ropes in this manner. They could also be made by jacking up a wagon wheel, tying the hide to one of the spokes and around the hub, and letting the wheel turn. After we had finished this rawhide rope, we made a collar for the antelope by taking a piece of rawhide, doubling one end several times, splitting a hole in the doubled end, and running the other end through the hole in the doubled end, thus making a knot. After cutting off the corners of the doubled end, we cut a hole in the other end, slipped the knotted end through this, and so had a collar from a piece of rawhide. We used to make hobbles and bridle reins in the same way.

We put the collar on the antelope, attached the long rawhide rope to the collar, and tied one end of the rope to a peach tree in the orchard. The antelope got the long rope around one of the bee gums and upset it. The bees soon covered him, and Grandma sent me to straighten out the fracas. The bees stung me on my head, face, hands, and my bare feet. Both my eyes were soon swollen shut. Before they became entirely closed, I got the antelope to the creek, but it was a fight to get him there and into the water. After I got him into the water, the bees left and he cooled off. I stripped off my clothes and applied the same treatment.

Grandma was my teacher while I lived with her, for there was no school nearer than Duncanville, a distance of six miles. Then Dad asked that I return home to Abilene, so Grandma took me to Dallas, bade me good-by, and put me on the westbound Texas and Pacific train.

Once again I was at home with my people, but I missed Grandma and all the fun we had together. Dad still had the leased ranch, and we moved out there for the summer, returning to Abilene in the fall so we kids could attend school. Dad ran horses on this ranch and kept all brother Judge's horses until he sold them. He had a large, fenced pasture, and there must have been a section of land where he ran a bunch of brood mares. Addie and I had about fifteen or twenty little Mexican burros at our home in Abilene. We had an eight- or ten-acre fenced pasture where we would bring the burros we had broken and later sell them to city children in Abilene.

We had one burro we just couldn't ride, and we decided to break him to drive. We made a harness with breastband and strap over his back and belly so we could hold it on him. We had a stick for a singletree, two straps of cowhide fastened to the breast-band for tugs, and we hitched these tugs to the singletree, which fastened to a cowhide that served as a cart. We made him a bridle with rawhide reins, and we had a sharp stick with a nail in the end with which to prod him to make him travel. We were sitting on the cowhide, thinly clad, no underwear, and when the burro saw the mares in the pasture, he ran to join them, but the hide got so hot we had to fall off. He crossed the coulee and got through the fence to the mares with this hide flapping and stampeded every mare through the fence, with the jack after them.

Dad was over in the pasture, riding a big bay horse with a bald face, but we hadn't seen him. He always rode a double-rigged saddle and carried a long rawhide rope tied to its horn. He knew very well we kids were into mischief trying to drive that jack, and he headed right for the coulee. I stuck up my head, and when he saw me, we took off for the house, but he was soon right behind us, pulling that rawhide rope down over us every time our feet hit the ground.

Near our home in Abilene there was a church for colored people. The other boys and myself tied a milch cow's calf, almost a yearling, to the bell cord. The bell hung outside the church, and during the service, when the congregation began to sing, we led the calf back and forth, causing the bell to ring loudly. All the folks inside were alarmed and ran out to see what was causing the bell to ring, but we had made our getaway, leaving our evidence behind us.

One evening we played another prank on the colored folks. This was at an old log church built on a hillside. Outside there was an opening where anyone could crawl under the building. The boy who played this prank was Herschel Anderson, a storekeeper's son. Before the service began, Herschel climbed up into the belfry and must have stayed up there an hour before the colored preacher opened the service, giving a sermon on living a good Christian life and loving God.

"If you don't follow along this path, the Devil will sho' git you," he shouted.

About this time Herschel spoke from the belfry, saying, "I'se comin' down an' git you right now."

That was the end of the church service that evening as the congregation fled.

The next spring, my sister Ida married Sam Gentry. After their marriage they left for Dallas, where they lived several years. With Ida gone from home, there were only Dad, Addie, Esther, and myself. Then Dad informed us one day that he was going to marry again. The girls told him that if he did, they would leave home, as they didn't want another stepmother. Dad told them he was deadly serious about remarrying, so they left for Dallas to live with our sister Mrs. Al Cornelius.

Two or three months later, Dad married a widow with three children, all my seniors. As soon as I could, I went down to the depot and hopped a freight for Dallas. The train crew were kind to me, and took up a collection of money so that I could buy a ticket and continue my trip by passenger train after reaching the end of their division. But it wasn't long until Dad came to Dallas and took me home again.

Dad's new wife had a small ranch halfway between Merkel and Trent, and they decided to move out there and make her place their home. Dad insisted that I make my home with them. I knew this would never work out, but what else could a poor kid do? Dad was now engaged in shipping horses to Arkansas and Louisiana, trading them for cattle, then shipping them back to Texas.

One evening while he was away from home, my stepbrothers gave me a terrible beating because I wouldn't do everything they wanted me to do. Most of it was bad, and I didn't want to get into trouble and so refused to carry out their orders. I slept in an old root cellar away from the house, as they wouldn't allow me to sleep in the house. After they beat me, I stayed in this root cellar for two days. When I could walk around and mount a horse, I made up my mind I'd leave. I owned two horses, one a pack horse, the other a saddle horse.

One night after everyone had gone to bed, I went to a small pasture we called the "catch all," caught the horses, put my saddle on the saddle horse first, then packed the other one with what bedding I had. I had no chance to get any grub, but I started south and rode all night. At daybreak I stopped in a coulee, inspected the pack horse, picketed him, and hobbled my saddle horse. I was twelve years old at this time. Tired, hungry, and homeless, I lay down to sleep while the horses grazed. The sun was high when I awoke. I was sure hungry, for I had eaten very little the previous day and had nothing to eat now. There was nothing to do but saddle up, throw the pack on the pack horse, and move on.

When I'd gone a few miles farther, I came to a ranch house. I told the lady that I was hungry and asked her if I might have something to eat. She made some corn-meal and white-flour griddle cakes and cooked a big juicy steak. Did this ever taste good! I asked for coffee, but she said I was too young to drink that beverage and gave me some milk. I stayed there an hour or two. The lady was curious to know where I was going, but I didn't take her into my confidence, for she would be sure to tell my father when he came along looking for me. She gave me a generous supply of grub and a frying pan, and I thanked her and went on my way again.

CHAPTER IV

With 'Rhome Shield

For the next three days I rode south, stopping only to cook and rest the horses and myself. My next stop was San Angelo, Texas, and upon reaching there I pulled into an old livery stable on the banks of the Concho River and told the livery man I was looking for a job.

"I'll take you up to see 'Rhome Shield," he said.

"Who's 'Rhome Shield?" I asked.

"Well, son," he replied, "'Rhome Shield is the sheriff of this county."

He took me up to Mr. Shield's house, and luckily we found him at home.

"Where're you from?" he asked.

"I won't tell you until I'm better acquainted," I replied. "If you give me a job and after I've worked for you awhile, then I'll tell you."

"Can you ride? Say, some colts?" he asked.

"I could sure try," I answered. "I've ridden all my life."

"Well," he said, "I'll give you a chance and try you out."

He then told me to go get my horses and bring them to his pasture. I never regretted hiring out to Mr. Shield, for his was a wonderful family. He was sheriff of Tom Green County at the time and was quite famous in the records of Texas. He was a terror to violators of the law, and when he went after a man, he brought him in, dead or alive.

Shield was a rancher until elected in 1888 to the office of hide and animal inspector, an important office in those days. After four years of unusual efficiency in this office, he was elected sheriff of the county, polling about 1,700 votes to his opponent's 162, and he held this office four consecutive terms before retiring to become a rancher again. He married a Miss Emma Emerick on May 22, 1891, and after forty-one years of happy marriage, died in his sleep on January 3, 1932, at the age of sixty-nine. But he will long be remembered as the nemesis of lawbreakers, breaking up bands of cow thieves, capturing the robbers of the Santa Fe train which was held up at Coleman Junction in 1898, and sending many other criminals to the penitentiary.

Mrs. Shield had a brother whose name was Frank Emerick. Frank made his home with the Shield family, and he was a few years my senior. Mr. Shield had a bunch of colts pastured near town, and we had a fine time halterbreaking these high-strung animals.

I'll always remember the colored fellow who worked for Mr. Shield. His name was Jerry, and he loved to play horse with us kids. He'd get down on all fours and buck hard and high—just like a real bronc. I can still see him, dressed in his blue jeans, with suspenders, and his hickory shirt. We'd get hold of his collar with one hand, the other in his suspenders, and believe me, he could sure buck. On one occasion he threw Frank, so we decided to get even. I was still only a kid and didn't stop to reason. Now Mr. Shield had some light race spurs made for us with star rowels, so I put on a pair of these. I nodded to Frank to keep still, mounted Jerry, and got my two holds.

"Are you ready?" Jerry hollered.

He had a trick of jumping just as high as he could, then throwing himself sideways. When he hollered, I dug in with those spurs and he jumped high, falling over backwards on top of me.

"My God, chile, what'd you have on?" he yelled.

28

A spur with a many-pointed rowell would not have hurt him, but the star spur has only a few points and they dig in. This unkind act of ours marked the end of all our fun, as Jerry would never play horse with us again. But he was loyal and didn't tell on us.

Mr. Shield had two bloodhounds which Jerry had trained for him. He'd tell Jerry to pull out from home, and he would then turn the dogs loose. Jerry always forgot about the dogs following him and once went to a Negro sporting house in San Angelo. This house had an outside stairway. The hounds trailed Jerry around town, then to this house, where he was upstairs dancing with a colored girl. The dogs grabbed him and he jumped up on a table to get away from them. They had to send word to Mr. Shield to come get his dogs before Jerry could get down.

I stayed at Mr. Shield's house for more than a year, mainly because I could speak Spanish. This helped Mrs. Shield, for many of the hired hands couldn't speak English. I'd learned Spanish from my father's Mexican help. A Mexican on Dad's old Sweetwater ranch had taught me how to make beautiful horsehair bridles, and also some saddle work. I knew horses and a swell outfit when I saw one, and I set about collecting the makings of a good outfit.

When I left Mr. Shield, I went to work for Mr. Stiles on the High Lonesome Ranch at the foot of the plains, almost due west of San Angelo. I stayed there about a year, until Mr. Shield and Tankersly bought this ranch. Mr. Shield again hired me, and I stayed on.

Looking back, I recall that he was a big man, big in build and in heart, too. He had a daughter and three sons, one named after himself, and no one ever called either anything except 'Rhome, short for Jerome. His wife came out to live on this ranch, and since most of the hands were Mexican, Mrs. Shield didn't trust

them too much. I stayed with them this time for two years. My job was to ride fence and grease the windmills, and I was really happy here.

Often Mexican riders got into serious fights, though when they were sober, they not only respected but feared Mr. Shield, their employer. But when they got drunk, they'd fight over almost anything—horses, saddles and gear, money or *señoritas*. They were quick on the draw and had red-hot tempers. Yet they were usually happy people, singing, dancing, and playing their guitars.

One day when Mr. Shield took me into San Angelo, we heard the sound of gunfire as we approached town, and there sitting in the middle of the street was a drunken Mexican. He was trying to kill everyone in sight, and wouldn't give up his arms. After trying all the methods he knew, Mr. Shield was forced to drop him cold. Such deadly gunplay was very serious, but kids of my day were accustomed to it. We knew how to handle guns with respect and caution.

The Ketchum boys, Tom and Sam, sometimes rode by Mr. Shield's ranch. They'd stick pieces of cedar between the barbed wire of the fences to let me know they were around. They usually had some other fellow with them. There was a cabin on the range where these fellows sometimes holed up, and they'd leave grub there for future use.

The Ketchums also had a brother-in-law who lived in San Angelo. He was a cowman, and I was well acquainted with his wife. These were fine, law-abiding folks and had no sympathy for their brothers' acts. Tom and Sam Ketchum, with some other outlaws, held up a train near Folsom, New Mexico, and Sam was shot and shortly died of his wounds. Later Tom attempted to hold up this same train alone and had his arm practically shot off. He was captured, taken to prison at Santa Fe, and later tried in Clayton. He was sentenced to hang, and the officers wanted absolute proof of his identity. He told them to bring 'Rhome Shield and 'Rhome could tell them who he was. Mr. Shield went to Clayton, where Tom shook hands with him.

The Ketchum boys, Berry, Sam, and Tom, were born on Richland Creek in western San Saba County, Texas, but their father, Dr. Ketchum, later moved his family to Tom Green County and settled at Knickerbocker, some twenty miles southwest of San Angelo. Sheriff Shield knew these boys well, as he did the toughs they ran around with, such men as Will Carver and Ben Kilpatrick, who later made a reputation of their own.

When Sam Ketchum died on July 24, 1899, at Santa Fe, Sheriff Shield, with Berry Ketchum, went out there to identify him, and now here he was again, going out to Clayton to identify Tom. On the morning of April 26, 1901, Tom Ketchum was to be hanged at eight o'clock, but a spurious telegram purporting to be from Governor Otero was received, asking for a delay until that afternoon. By the time it was discovered that this telegram was a fake, Tom's life had been prolonged for five hours.

A priest came into Tom's cell and asked him if he wished him to pray for him, but Tom cursed the priest and said, "I'll know more about Heaven and Hell in the next few minutes than you will."

It was just a little after one o'clock in the afternoon when Tom was led from his cell to the gallows by Sheriff García and several deputies. He was a cool customer and did not seemed concerned. He calmly took his place upon the trap without assistance. The hangman's noose was placed about his neck, and he even assisted in adjusting it.

The sheriff raised his ax, it fell upon the rope that held up the trap door, and Black Jack, as Tom had come to be known, shot downward. The drop was so great that, instead of his neck being broken, his whole head was jerked off. It was a most gruesome sight.

There was an old ranch woman down on Devils River where Tom sometimes made his headquarters, and he had told me this old woman had a gun of his and he wished me to have it. I wrote her and requested the gun, but never received an answer.

While I was working for Mr. Shield, two men and a woman came to San Angelo. They bought a team and spring wagon. The woman's husband was supposed to be in poor health—said he had t.b. This fellow carried a large life-insurance policy. They told everyone they were going down into the Devils River country to see if he could regain his health. The Devils River country is southwest of San Angelo about seventy-five miles and is a very rough, rugged country.

The man's wife and the other fellow later returned, saying her husband had died and they had buried him down there. The wife then put in a claim for the insurance, but the insurance company became suspicious. The widow had told them where her husband was buried. Mr. Shield was sent to look into this, and he took Bronc Dreenan and myself along. We found the grave all right, but there was nothing buried in it except some burnt wood. Later the Cross-Tie roundup outfit picked up a fellow walking across country who answered the description of the missing man. They took him to the sheriff's office, where he was proved to be the woman's husband.

Another little story I remember concerns a Mexican who wanted a driving horse, a single driver for a cart. He came to Mr. Shield's house to see if he'd sell him such a horse, and Mr. Shield showed him a well-broken little chestnut sorrel and the Mexican bought him. This Mexican lived across the Concho River at the old fort. A few days after this horse deal, Mr. Shield and I went up the Four-Cross-L Ranch to bring in an old Mexican who had lost his mind. When we were coming back, we saw this Mexican horse buyer's horse dragging the shafts of his cart. We got out of the buckboard, caught the horse, and were leading him back to San Angelo when we came across the angry Mexican and what was left of his cart. He was plenty mad and gave Mr. Shield a good cussin' in Spanish. Though Mr. Shield was one of the most fearless sheriffs Texas ever had, this incident only amused him, and he told the Mexican he would give him another horse and buy him a new cart.

CHAPTER V

More Wanderings

WHEN I LEFT the employ of Mr. Shield, I went to work for the Four-Cross-L, on the Concho River about thirty-five miles due west of San Angelo. I was a wrangler for the roundup. Another kid, Hugh Roberts, was working there, too. He was just about my age and his home was in Abilene. We rode after cattle, too, as well as hunted up the horses belonging to the different riders for the roundup.

Along the Concho River the hills were dotted with clumps of cedar and mesquite. It was an interesting place along those sheltered bluffs, for there was much Indian picture writing. Hugh and I used to study these by the hour when we had time, and we liked to camp here in order to look at them. Other riders and travelers who chanced this way also found time to stop and wonder at them.

These writings were done on the rocks, in red mostly, but there were some in orange and black and white. Most of them were symbols of some sort, often devils with tails. Many thought them to be messages concerning the condition of the country as to food, hunting, and water supply. Perhaps you've wondered how a person can remember all this after so many years, but it's the way one is impressed at the time. In our work as range men, the landmarks and country about us were important. It is no fun to be lost or unable to locate cattle or horses. A person makes it a study. Everything becomes important. We were there so long and had nothing else much to think about, so we tried to figure out these pictures. It never occurred to me to add anything to them, and besides, we didn't have any of the earth paints or whatever they used. Sometimes we did carve brands on the rocks though.

I worked at the Four-Cross-L for two and a half years. Bronc Dreenan was foreman of this outfit. He was a tall Texan, hump shouldered, redheaded, with a freckled face, and he always spoke of me as his boy. When we shipped trainloads of cattle out of San Angelo, he'd always get drunk. In those days storekeepers would set big tubs of eggs outside on the sidewalk. Bronc got drunk one day and staggered into a tub of these eggs. This made him mad and he went on the prod. He jumped into the tub of eggs and began breaking them in fine style. A clerk came out of the store and told him to leave.

"Not till I finish breaking these eggs," replied Bronc, at the same time throwing several at the clerk.

The storekeeper came out pretty riled up and demanded that Bronc pay for the eggs.

"I've had a good time breaking your eggs," answered Bronc, "and I'll pay for 'em, so you won't be out a nickel."

We then went back to the Four-Cross-L range, gathered up another trainload of cattle, and shipped them out of San Angelo. When we shipped carloads of cattle, two cowhands worked inside the corral to cut cattle and run them into the stockcar. Bronc asked me to help with the work. Being the foreman of the outfit, he was always in the corral to see that the work was properly handled. He always called me Kennon and never addressed me by my first name. One day two of my brothers-in-law, Joe and Sam Gentry, were sitting on the top rail of the corral watching us work the cattle. One of them called me over.

"Are you Bob Kennon?" he asked, and I said I was.

"Do you know who we are?" he then asked me.

"Yes," I answered, "you're my brothers-in-law, the Gentrys."

Then they told me they lived in San Angelo and asked me to come see their families. This I did, but I couldn't stay long, for the wagon was pulling back to the ranch again.

Suggs and Tankersly were the owners of the Four-Cross-L Ranch. Suggs always had a lot of hogs. They would run up and down the river just like wild hogs. Every so often he would gather up a bunch of them and sell them off in carload lots.

They soon sold this ranch to a titled Englishman whose family wished to get him away from England, as he drank heavily. This young Englishman came to take over his holdings, bringing several of his friends with him. He was to receive one hundred dollars per month from the parents of each of these young fellows if he would teach them the cow business. Since there were seven or eight of them, he must have raked in a tidy sum each month.

Suggs and Tankersly gathered all the cattle and horses from the range and pasture. It took about a month to complete the work before they could turn them over to the new owners. On the ranch there was a big horse pasture in which was a high knoll. We counted the cattle around this knoll. This finished, we began counting the horses the same way. They ran the horses around once and were starting a second time. There was a pinto, a bald-faced sorrel with white spots, in the bunch, and one of the young fellows spotted him and yelled that he'd been by before. Lord Anderson, the new owner, and Bronc Dreenan got into a hot argument over this. Dreenan finally said he wouldn't argue further about the matter and suggested that they flip a coin and split the difference. Both agreed to this.

All these Englishmen wore heavy, horn-rimmed glasses with large rims almost to their eyebrows and halfway down their cheeks. Where the glasses fit behind the ears they had straps attached and fastened with a buckle at the back of the head to hold them tightly in place. This sure did amuse me, for it gave them a

Branding for the 72 Bar, owned by Ma Hamilton. The cowboys liked her because she was a good boss.

A chuck wagon, with cowboys enjoying their grub in its shade. Bob
Kennon is the fourth man from the left (wearing tall, white hat
and eating sandwich).

very owlish appearance. None of these fellows smoked or chewed tobacco.

I worked for these Englishmen about six months. They didn't feed their hands as Suggs and Tankersly did, and we had no more cake and pie. Neither did we have any more beefsteaks, as they wouldn't kill a beef, but fed us pork. I was used to plenty of good beefsteak, so this didn't suit me. These English fellows didn't eat with us cowhands either, but cooked for themselves in another house on the ranch.

Sometimes Lord Anderson would go out on inspection trips over the range and he would ask me to accompany him. One day we were riding up the river and he said he'd forgotten his silver drinking cup, which he always tied under the throat-latch of his bridle.

"I'm very dry," he said.

"Lie down and drink out of the river," I told him.

"Oh, I cannot lie down and drink like a horse," he replied.

Bronc told me that when I was out with Lord Anderson, to tell him nothing, give him no advice, nor try to educate him in any way. "The less you say to him, the better off we'll be," he'd say.

When we were working the herd, Lord Anderson would have one of the men from the ranch hitch a team to a big three-seated spring wagon and bring all these English fellows out to the range so they could observe how roping and branding was done. None of them ever attempted to take an active part in any of this work, for Bronc wouldn't tolerate any foolishness. Lord Anderson kept these fellows busy most of the time digging postholes, building fences, putting up hay, and other such labor under the supervision of a boss.

As I've stated before, we only worked for this English outfit six months, that is, Bronc and myself. We both quit. Lord Anderson offered us a raise in pay, which we both refused. Bronc had not seen his folks for years, so he went home to Brownsville and I never saw him again. I struck out for Midland and got a job with the Cross-Tie outfit.

I'd written my friend Hugh Roberts to come join me and we'd work and see the country together. He had a good home and steady parents who had always looked after him, but he wanted to see what the outside world was like.

We began wandering around and working at different outfits, a short time in each place. We went to the Cross-Tie in the Big Spring country. In the years before the big drought came, it was the finest cow country you could want. It had everything: fine, tall grass, water, and shelter. I'm glad I was gone before the sod-busters came along. They were sure the ruination of the cattle country. We soon got tired of the Cross-Tie and went to the Turkey Track, where we spent a few weeks.

It was getting toward fall roundup time, and we drifted on farther west. We decided to hit for the home ranch of the Millett outfit and ask the boss for a job. We ate first and believed we were hired, but after dinner the old man told us he didn't want us on his payroll, as we were no good. Just "grub-liners," he called us, "no-good roamers" and a lot of other names. He charged us fifty cents each, too, for the dinner. This was the limit and the worst insult a person could receive. No one ever charged for food or shelter in those days. Hospitality was the custom of all the West, and it was certainly unusual to find anyone so stingy.

He must have known, too, that we were nearly broke. We paid for our meal and left the ranch, two of the maddest cowpunchers you ever saw. We burned the wind getting away from there. Old Millett's ears must have burned with the cussin' we gave him.

As we rode along, Hugh had a sudden good idea. "Let's double back and have some fun at the old skinflint's expense," he said.

We rode back a ways and picked up some of Millett's cattle, cutting out a fine three-year-old steer. We tied him down and made a greasewood fire. With a cinch ring and a couple of green sticks, we put a new brand on this steer right beneath Millett's brand: MEALS 50¢ This steer never did seem to get shipped out, and ran the range for years. Riders often told us they saw this brand when they worked that section. It was a hell of a good piece of walking advertising.

Hugh got pretty homesick at times and so did I, but we wouldn't admit it. I felt I'd just started and I told him I wasn't going back until I had a better outfit and a pocketful of money to show my ornery stepbrothers. I made up my mind I was going to show the folks some presents and the fellows in the bunkhouses at home just what a roll I had, and how I'd clean them out when I got back. We'd lie out under the stars and talk about all this, never admitting that we wished we were home. We were still only kids, but when daylight came, we were back on the job with the cattle.

Later we drifted into Pecos. This town was a small place but lively enough when the cowpunchers came in. It was mostly desert country around there, yet the Pecos Valley was wide and had good grass, water, and good camping places. There were some high mountaintops rising up out there, too, and they made some grand pictures of all this country and put them on tourists' folders. It was a country of mountains, rivers, desert, and sky. There were no big herds of cattle here. We left the cattle sometimes and sneaked into Pecos Town. This little old burg was a badman's town for sure, as it had a terrible reputation. It still lives in books and movies, though I laugh at the way they handle some of the gunplay and the stunts the desperadoes in the movies pull off.

We left the cattle one afternoon and went into town. On the way in, my horse threw a shoe, and this slowed us up a bit. We went in peaceful and quiet, planning to have some shoeing done on the horses while we had some fun in town. The town was quiet when we got there—"damned quiet," Hugh remarked. There wasn't a soul in sight: the streets were deserted. No horses at the hitchrack. It looked funny to me.

The blacksmith was lounging in the shade of his shop, smoking, as we rounded the building. He got up so fast he nearly bumped into the wall, held a gun on us, and kept threatening us, especially Hugh. We had a hell of a time making him understand that we were not gunmen. Later he told us that Hugh had better disguise himself, for he was the image of a gunman who had just shot up the place and killed some gamblers the day before.

Hugh was a tall fellow, well over six feet, and he had flaming red hair. It had grown pretty long, and it seems the killer had long red hair, too. This scared us pretty bad, and we had the smithy go to the saloon with us and get the saloonkeeper, the town's barber, to cut Hugh's hair.

When we'd filled up and forgotten about the excitement, we went to the hotel cafe to eat. The saloonkeeper was so drunk by now that Hugh was afraid to trust him with the scissors and razor. There was a big woman at the cafe and she cut hair when this barber fellow was on one of his drunks, which seemed to be pretty often. Hugh started putting up a kick and tried to get out before she came back with the scissors, but I wouldn't let him because I was afraid we'd never get out of town alive if any more people took us for these two gunmen of the day before. Maybe you think she didn't make a good job of cutting Hugh's hair; she damned near cut him bald. I was going to have her trim me up, too, but after I saw what she'd done to him I got cold feet, and we just bought some grub and went for our horses.

We were lucky, too, for as we headed out toward the foothills and began to climb a little, we could see the biggest cloud of dust kicked up from the trail below. They were horsemen coming at a fast gait, badmen no doubt, or gunfighting cowboys chasing or being chased.

It was nearing the fall roundup again and we decided to drift on farther. We'd been planning to go to El Paso, but Hugh was getting real homesick by this time, and tired of a life of wandering. We'd drifted toward Sierra Blanca, a little town on the Texas and Pacific Railroad, and stopped at a section house three or four miles east of the town. A cook there fed us, after which we rode into town. It was not much of a place, a store and depot as I remember. We went into the store and found a redheaded lady working there.

"Aren't you little Bobby Kennon?" she asked me.

"That's what I am," I answered, "but how did you know me?"

"We were your parents' neighbor in Merkel at the time your mother died," she replied.

She was very kind and asked us to spend some time with them and rest before going farther, but we both thanked her and said we'd have to be going on. Now Hugh was more homesick than ever to see his folks. We had talked of going down into Old Mexico as we rode along together, but he backed down when I said we should winter in El Paso and then look for a spread across the Río Grande.

Hugh now decided to go home, and we said good-by. Our trails never crossed again. Mine widened out and out, and toward a different world than the one Hugh and I had known.

I always did love a black horse, and I had a beauty, a single-footer named Peacock. He could travel like the wind and had the best endurance I ever saw in a horse. Everybody was trying to make a deal to get hold of him. They even tried to win him as a stake in a gambling game. I couldn't part with him, for we had been pals so long.

It happened later, though, that things got tough for me, putting me in a tight place, and one day while drinking, I sold him to a fellow who ran a livery stable in a little town east of El Paso. Now if you know just how livery-stable horses were treated by the men who hired them, you'd understand just how drunk and desperate I must have been to put this grand animal in their cruel and careless establishment.

I got a lot of money for him and was having one grand time when we all got into a fight. Some Mexicans cut up a fellow pretty bad and we heard he was dying. The town marshal got after our bunch and told us to leave town pronto. Well, I had no horse, so what was I to do? There was only one thing I could think of. I sneaked in the side door of the livery barn and gave a low whistle to Peacock. He answered me with a whinny. The barn man was cleaning out a far stall.

"What you want?" he called out.

"Just taking my horse," I answered.

For all he knew, or seemed to care, this was all right, as he didn't know I had sold the horse to his boss. I lost no time saddling up, and rode out of town as if all hell was at our heels.

I rode all night, straight up the Río Grande. When morning came, I was weak from hunger, but happy. Here I was with my old pal Peacock back in my possession. I met a fellow coming up from an arroyo and thought sure he was after me, but he proved to be the owner of a big spread and was out looking for stray horses. He asked me if I wanted a job and when I told him I did, we went on to his ranch, the Diamond A, and there I had the best breakfast I ever tasted. No one asked me any questions, but it was still too close to trouble so I drew my wages after the first month and hit the trail again.

I never felt easy about Peacock, for horse stealing was a crime and I didn't have any hankering for jails, nor ropes about my neck, and so I made a fast getaway into Old Mexico, arriving at Cananea. No one made any trouble over the horse, so I got a job braking ore wagons on those steep hillside roads. I had to jump from one wagon to the next and set the brakes, and woe to you if you missed your footing. But I didn't like this job too well, and after four days I took Peacock and rode back into Texas.

I continued to worry about Peacock and sold him again to a rancher who was a horse lover and who promised to take real good care of him. I then bought a pinto, and knowing the world was wide, I rode into it looking for new adventures. I added to my string of horses on the way and had several good ones.

CHAPTER VI

To El Paso and West

I HEADED toward El Paso, as it seemed the thing to do. I had to lay off for the winter somewhere and thought this would be a good place to stay. It would be a good place to start from, too, in the spring, for near-by ranchers came here to hire riders for the spring work. Now I had heard all the stories connected with El Paso for years, and it seemed as if you'd never been around if you'd never been to El Paso. The talk in the bars over West Texas was "El Paso ... El Paso." So it was with great expectations that I arrived in town. I had a little money, but with the pace of that town I was soon broke and had to sell my horses.

A fellow from Big Spring had given me all the dope on El Paso before I got there, and I thanked my stars I wasn't too much of a green kid when I arrived, even if I was just a kid in age. It was hard, at that time, for one to realize just how dangerous this town could be.

I remember pretty well how it looked the first day I laid eyes on it. There were scraggly looking peaks to the north and west; to the east there were low, dry plains and the mesas. The Sierra Madres came back into the valley south and west across the river. El Paso itself lay just under a peak which had an Indian name. As I remember, it was called Comanche Mountain Peak. Anyway, it was an unusual sight. Back in the days of 1849, when they were having a lot of travel, the old Butterfield Stage Line had run through here. They claimed it to be the longest mail route in the whole world. It was a long way from St. Louis to Frisco.

In El Paso I grew up overnight, you might say. The thing to do was to stay out of trouble and keep the best and safest company you could. A few of us learned to stick together, and we managed to have a good time. I never saw so much useless killing. Mexicans would get drunk and come over the river to find some fun. They killed over cards, women, horses, or just plain orneryness I reckon. They were plumb loco when they got whiskey; just like the Indians up there in Montana, except they were better with a gun and knife.

I'll admit I was no angel, but I kept out of serious trouble. We had our own system of knowing how to avoid these fellows, either white or Mexican, who came in just spoiling for trouble. A lot of money changed hands that winter over the bars and tables. It was the widest-open town I'd ever seen. There was any kind of game you wanted: faro, monte, poker, dice. There was no law recognized as such, for the sheriffs were all asleep or supposed to be continually out after bandits.

Dead bodies were disposed of in short order without prayer or service of any kind. In fact, I don't think there was a padre or sky-pilot of any faith there when I spent the winter. No one was interested in marryings or buryings. Things just happened as they did, and nature took its course.

The town had gotten wilder and rougher as the railroads came into the valley of the Río Grande. These were the Southern Pacific and the Texas and Pacific. Often desperadoes had good hide-outs in the near-by hills and came into town at night under cover of disguise. They'd gamble and win a pile to keep themselves along the trail the next day.

I met an old schoolmate of mine in El Paso, a fellow named Joe Gardikee, with whom I'd gone to school in Abilene. Joe was a patrolman on the bridge at El Paso on the American side. A Mexican broke out of jail one night and the Mexican police were after him. He ran across the bridge, shooting at the Mexican

45

officers. They returned the fire, and Joe and I thought the lead was flying too thick. We crawled down on the approach of the bridge and let the Mexicans shoot it out.

Joe got me a job with a packing outfit. They packed about two hundred burros each day, packing supplies and grub to the mines at Cananea. They'd pack ore back to El Paso on the return trip. I understood packing and liked the work and stayed with this job two months. When the packers packed the burros, they'd cinch the packsaddles very tight, cinch them about three times, and yell *"Bueno,"* which, as you know, means "good" in Spanish.

Every day while we were packing, a young boy would come to watch us. He never talked to anyone or made himself a nuisance. When we had finished the packing, he would leave. One day a well-bred gentleman came to where we were packing and asked if a young boy had been coming there.

"Oh, yes," someone answered, "he does, but never makes any trouble. Just seems to be interested in the packing."

"I have an amusing story to tell you packers," said the gentleman. "The boy is my son. His mother was lacing his sister into a corset, and he was looking on at the proceedings. Everything was coming along just great with the fitting when he shouted: 'Good work, Ma. Cinch her three times, then holler *"Bueno."* ' "

One day just about daylight, two gunmen finished out an old score. Later we found out that one had spent a couple of years searching for the other, whom he'd sworn to kill on sight. The other, whose name I didn't know, was a big fellow who had been hiding in El Paso all winter. He kept clear of the bars, though he did a little gambling now and then in public. He wore long hair and a dark, heavy beard. This was no doubt worn for disguise.

Just the night before this shooting a man rode into town and hung around all evening with a bunch of Mexicans. He had a tip that this was the place to find his man. The news spread quickly that a gang of gunfighters were watching the roads and outlying streets so that no one could leave without their knowing it.

A couple of us fellows were staying in a bachelor diggings with an old cowman. We were about broke and just hanging on until we could get another job. It was at the end of the street and there were a lot of adobe houses cluttered at the far side. Beyond this there was a small stable where one could hire livery horses.

At the sound of shooting, everyone woke up and started for his own six-shooter, though heaven knows shots were common enough, often only some fool in a playful mood. But at this hour we were aware things were pretty hot and close at hand.

The barn man said afterward that this hunted man with the beard had sneaked in to hire a horse the previous night, but he didn't dare leave, as there was such a close watch on things. He made a deal for a horse, intending to sneak out at dawn and make his getaway. There had been so much drinking among the bunch that he hoped they would let up watching him so closely. But he was followed and shot just as he rounded the adobe wall near the barn. Some tall, slim fellow kept plugging him long after he was a corpse. He must have had a terrible grudge against him. Then he simply rode off on a sorrel horse which one of his Mexican friends had been holding close by. No one challenged him, and no sheriff was in sight to halt him. We stood at the door, unable to do a thing. After he had gone, we mixed in with the crowd at the bar, but very little was said, as this cold-blooded killing had left us speechless.

I had about all I wanted of El Paso, and when a bunch of cowmen and their foremen rode into town looking for ranch hands, I was quick to offer myself for a job. It was then I met Mr. Paramore, of Paramore and Merchant, bankers from Abilene, Texas, who had big ranches in Arizona. I went with him, glad to get out of El Paso.

It was grand out there at the ranch in Lonesome Valley in Arizona. It was a big spread and lay on the west side of the

47

Chiricahua Mountains. I stayed there the rest of the season, and the folks were certainly wonderful. The old settlers could tell some terrible tales about the Apache raids they had experienced.

While working for Paramore and Merchant, whose ranch was near Bisbee, I met Sol Schooner, a faro-bank dealer and gambler at the Red Dog Gambling House. This was a big adobe building, with a saloon downstairs and gambling rooms upstairs. I had known Schooner in San Angelo, where his wife and family still made their home.

Two tall holdup men wearing masks and kid gloves held up the Red Dog. They made us turn our faces to the wall and said no one would be hurt if we kept quiet. These two gents then proceeded to scoop all the money into sacks, carried the sacks downstairs, and made their getaway. It was several minutes before anyone stirred, then all kinds of guns came into view. One fellow slid down a porch pillar to the street to notify police.

On another occasion, two brothers came riding into Bisbee and held up a saloon. When they were leaving, someone shot the horse out from under one of them. The other rode back and picked up his brother, then galloped out of town.

On my visits to Douglas I found that the Mexicans played monte on the sidewalks. Should the weather be a little chilly, they would build a small fire to warm their hands. They were always smoking cigarettes, and always had a pot of chili, hot tamales, or some tortillas, which they would offer you in their kind way. Somehow I always admired the Mexican people for their great hospitality in their homes and their wonderful love for their children.

The next job I had was with the P Cross. I worked there about a month and got fired. Then I went to work for the Shaw brothers, Jim and John, who ran the Boot outfit. Jim was married to a young girl who was very fond of fine driving horses. She had a rubber-tired buggy and could sure handle a buggy whip and make those horses step. She would take me with her and drive up and down the streets of Bisbee with those high-stepping horses. The Shaws were also fond of house cats. Once Jim was called to Tombstone for jury duty, and while he was gone, John decided to have more accommodations for the cats. They had one hole cut into the house, called the "cat hole," but John decided one wasn't enough. When I asked him why he cut another, he said: "Well, when the big cat's goin' in and out of that hole, there's no way for the smaller ones to go out, so I sawed another hole for them."

This amused me, but it was their house and I said nothing else about it. They were kind, generous, and good bosses, and I was very fond of all of them. After I'd worked for them all summer I decided I'd like to take a trip to Mexico City, but after taking in all the sights there I decided to come back to the States. On the train, in the seat in front of me, were two large women and a little boy. I couldn't keep from wondering at the peculiar shape of this boy and what was making him cry all the time. When we got to the border, the customs inspector looked over everyone's belongings before we crossed. After this duty was performed and the customs inspector had left, these women began undressing the little boy. They had smuggled yards and yards of silk wrapped around this little boy's body. This accounted for his queer shape and his constant crying.

I began looking for another job and found one with a man named Alec Gardiner. He had a son, Buster, and their ranch was near Bisbee in the Sulphur Springs Valley. Buster and I broke horses for a rancher who had an outfit at the foot of the Cherry-cows Mountains. These were horses which this fellow matched as teams, then broke and sold them to the stage lines. I was very much at home with the Gardiners, and they always called me Dogie. They were real down-to-earth people who dared to be themselves. Mrs. Gardiner had been born and raised in Tennessee and always used snuff. She had a border of snuff bottles along the walk to the door, and the flower beds were bordered with them too. Mr. Gardiner was a tall, thin man and didn't weigh more than 120 pounds, but he was an excellent jockey.

He took me with him to his brother's ranch at Stiles to get a carload of horses and other stuff—saddles, harness, etc. We were gone about ten days on this trip. The Gardiners had a fast race horse which they brought overland to run in the races at Bisbee on the Fourth of July. A saloon man in Bisbee also owned a fast racing stud which all the gamblers and sporting women swore by. They all declared no horse could beat him.

The Gardiners brought their horse from Stiles a week before the race, he and his wife coming overland in a covered wagon. The race horse was tied behind this wagon, and he looked like anything but a race horse. He had cockleburs and gumbo in his mane and tail, his tail being long with rough hair. It seems they did everything to make him look like a scrub. They put up their tent on the edge of town and made camp. Then Mr. Gardiner went into town asking if there were any race horses in Bisbee. He played like he was drunk. His wife was with him and kept telling him to keep his mouth shut. "You ain't got no race horse. You're just always shootin' off your face," she kept saying.

They were a pair of seedy-looking characters. He hadn't shaved for weeks and was wearing long, gray whiskers, with more tobacco juice on them than in his mouth. Mrs. Gardiner was wearing an old blue denim dress down to her shoe tops and one of those old slatted bonnets. She'd whittled out sticks of mesquite until they were smooth and put these in the bonnet so it would be stiff and not fall in her face and over her eyes.

They finally matched a horse race with this saloon man for five hundred dollars. Mrs. Gardiner had the money in one of those old leather saddlebags, the kind the early-day doctors carried to hold their medicine when they made calls.

"Dogie," she said to me, "you hold the sack open while I count out the money."

She would walk around with the moneybag in her hand, asking if anyone would like to bet. On the day of the race, they held things up as long as possible to get all the bets they could possibly add, but the saloon man's stud was still the favored one and bets were not hard to get.

When they couldn't stall any longer, Gardiner mounted his horse and, with the other jockey, went to the post. The race was on, and folks soon learned that this seedy-looking horse could just burn up the track. They found out the old man could ride, too. The sporting crowd lost their money, but they were good losers and the Gardiners were happy, for they knew all along that their horse could win.

They had a daughter named Rosie, and she had an admirer whom her dad didn't like because he thought him dishonest. This fellow wanted to ask Mr. Gardiner for his daughter, but he didn't want to go alone to do this. He begged me to go with him because he said I knew them so well.

When he asked for Rosie's hand in marriage, her dad replied: "I ain't got to live with her. Go and speak to her ma."

He made a speech to Rosie's mother and ended by saying: "I'll see that she never wants for wood and water."

"Yes," the mother replied, "wood on her back and water in her eyes."

But Rosie did marry this handsome scamp. They were industrious, and made money every way they could. They cut cordwood and hauled it to the mines at Bisbee. They put me to work driving a string team, and he drove another. One day I was working with old man Gardiner snaking wood down off a hillside when an old she-bear with two cubs came down off the mountains. The cubs came running to meet me and she right behind them. "Dogie," yelled old man Gardiner when he saw my plight, "turn that horse loose and climb up on that wagon if you don't want to get chawed up."

The Gardiners had a wood camp at a spring and a bunch of Mexicans resented them being there, for they claimed the spring, but Gardiner stood his ground. This resulted in a hot argument, and a shooting followed. Gardiner injured two Mexicans, one of them dying later in a hospital in Bisbee. The officers, however, didn't make any trouble for him nor his sons over this affair.

On one occasion the Rangers were out after Gardiner's son-in-law and I was with him. There was a big cut along the railroad, not far from Gardiner's house. The Rangers were on the north side of the tracks on Silver Creek, along the border of Arizona and Old Mexico. They were hot on our trail when he jumped off his horse and shot one of the Rangers, being himself protected from their fire by the railroad cut. He killed a horse from under another Ranger, who had picked up his companion, while we made our way to Gardiner's.

CHAPTER VII

Up the Trail to Montana

WHEN I LEFT the Gardiners, I decided to go back to El Paso for a spell. While there I met the wagon boss of the famous Terrazas Ranch in Old Mexico. He asked me if I'd like to go down there and work for the outfit. I was glad of the chance and took the job with this big spread that I'd heard of for so many years. I was only paid eighteen dollars per month, in Mexican money, and they had mighty poor grub, mostly chili beans and dried beef. I almost forgot what fresh beef tasted like.

Don Luis Terrazas, the cattle king of Chihuahua, was the largest landholder and cattle breeder in the world at that time. He owned about 1,000,000 head of cattle and branded as high as 200,000 calves in one year at one time. Before the revolution later broke him, he had over 3,000 head of horses in use on his more than 11,000,000 acres of ranches.

Mrs. Terrazas was a wonderful woman and was wealthy in her own right. She gave Don Luis eight daughters and five sons. Always friendly and charitable with their hired hands, she visited their various ranches with a coterie of servants in carriages. Their homes, both in the city of Chihuahua and on the main ranch, were like palaces, and many of the furnishings were from Europe.

All the buildings on the ranch where I worked were constructed of adobe, and there were so many of them it looked like a small town laid out in streets. The main hacienda was a long, low, rambling structure with wide eaves to keep out the sun and was surrounded by a big yard with beautiful flower beds, trees, and vines of all kinds.

Bill Nort, one of the foremen, gave me a job wrangling horses. He was a kindly sort of man who understood and could talk with a kid like me. Taking this job was the turning point of my life. I had only been working there a few months when Mr. Broadus and Mr. Hysham, two cowmen from Montana, together with their foreman, Mr. Baker, came down to buy steers.

They bought two thousand Mexican steers from Terrazas, and Baker was to trail them north to Montana. Baker asked Bill Nort and Tom Cottrell, a Terrazas cowhand, myself, and a few others to come along up the trail. I was willing and anxious to go up the cattle trail at any time. This had been my hope and dream for months. If a fellow had never been up to Montana on a cattle drive, he wasn't considered much of a cowman. I held back, though, until Mr. Broadus agreed to pay me a monthly wage of forty dollars for the trip. Compared with the eighteen dollars I was getting, this seemed like a fortune to me and I told him I'd go all the way.

All the marvelous yarns I'd heard in the bars and cafes about Montana came back to me, and we punchers were so excited that night we couldn't sleep. We wanted to go into the town near by and celebrate, but the new boss put it up to us in such a way that we changed our minds.

At last everything was in readiness, the cattle gathered, tallied, and turned over to Broadus and Hysham. With the transaction closed, the wagons loaded with supplies, beds, etc., and the cook fixed out with all his culinary needs, everything was complete for the long trip north. The remuda of horses was gathered, and every cowhand had his own saddle, chaps, and war-bag where he kept his personal belongings.

Early the next morning we crossed the Río Grande under Terrazas' supervision. After crossing into Texas, Broadus and

Hysham gave the orders. We didn't travel fast nor very far in a week's time, and camped at regular intervals, holding the steers on good feed all along the way. Cattle get footsore and leg weary if crowded too hard or handled roughly, and they wanted the steers to reach Montana in good condition.

Mr. Baker was a wonderful range man and our outfit seemed to be as complete as anyone could want. We had good chuck and a dandy cook whom we called Flapjack. If he had any other name, it didn't matter, for names were not important to men in those days. All we cared about was that he be a good cook and stay on the job. Most of the boys had nicknames. There was usually a reason for these names, and they fit and stuck. Cowboys were the wittiest fellows I ever knew, and were quick on the trigger with a joke and always full of mischief.

On the whole, ours was a good outfit, agreeable and happy go lucky. Tom Cottrell and I became close friends. We stuck together, and believe me, we helped each other out of many a tough spot during the long drive north. There was also a one-eyed half-breed Mexican who used to stand guard with me at night. Sometimes he'd sing to us, and he had a fine tenor voice. He knew how to sing to the herd, too, and seemed to have a knack of soothing them.

We had a fine run of luck and were having no serious trouble with the herd. Only the lightning storms caused any worry. We were bound to get these storms, for the weather was getting very hot. You may not know that cattle stampede like hell in a lightning storm. First, they hate the heat and closeness before it breaks, and the distant rumble gets them all worked up. Then the fierce lightning finishes the job. Amid the dust and confusion, even the men get short tempered and go to pieces. Many an old hand claimed that cowboys were likely to go crazy at this time, though few did. Most of them could stand the test; it was a part of their life. The first storm on this drive was the worst, for we didn't seem to be organized just right when it hit us and it came up so quickly out of nowhere.

After the first run, we did our best to get the cattle to milling. If unable to keep them from scattering too much, we would have to ride miles and miles to round them up the next morning, so everyone worked hard. It was a bad thing to have a herd scatter on you and have to spend days rounding them up again.

As quickly as it came up, the storm passed over, and we very luckily got the cattle quieted down. Night passed somehow, and in the morning we hit the trail north again. We had other storms less severe, and we controlled things better.

On our trek north there were a number of rivers to cross. Every crossing was another struggle to get the cattle to take water and swim. The southern rivers were wide and sluggish, but not so with the northern ones. These were swift, with high, steep banks and mostly with clear water except the Missouri, which is always muddy, having many sand bars and treacherous holes because of the constant shifting of its course.

There were other things to worry about, too. Bands of rustlers used to raid just such outfits as ours. They got away with plenty of trail stock and were well organized throughout the years after the first drives came up.

We had a scare one night when a couple of the boys came in and declared they had spotted a bunch of riders waiting for us at the water hole ahead. We were sure they were rustlers. We prepared to shoot it out with them if we had to, but with two thousand steers in our herd, we didn't want any shooting if it could be avoided. They were nowhere in sight when we reached the water hole, nor did we later encounter any of them. For this we thanked our lucky stars. They laid off of us for some good reason. Maybe they thought us just a little outfit until they saw our riders, or perhaps they were waiting for some other outfit, or a more favorable night. Rustlers had a slick way of stampeding a herd, or they would pick a favorable night and surprise the herders. We always doubled our night guard in a dangerous area.

When the grass was good, we trailed the cattle; when it was poor, we shipped them on the railroad until the grass country got better. Baker was a marvel at this and seemed to sense things. I'll say he was the most wonderful trail boss I ever saw, and I've known a lot of them in my years.

The trail we took had been carefully mapped and planned by experienced cattlemen who certainly knew their business. Our trail was like a long rope with its coils and twists, and its tangles were always straightened out. The route shied away from the beaten track near towns except where it was necessary, at certain points, to put the steers in the railway cars.

Once we were properly outfitted, we kept the trail. We thought of nothing but Montana, night and day. We bedded down the cattle at night and then at daylight again started the trek over the prairie. What a sight those old steers would make if we could see them again! Horns tossing as they swam the flood of a swollen stream, they made an unforgettable sight as we pressed on and on toward the north—and Powder River.

Kansas had some settlements along the way. The settlers' houses were made of sod. They'd take a plow and team, rip up long furrows of sod, cut this into lengths with a spade, and lay these sod lengths layer on layer, much as a child builds his house of blocks. They had dirt floors, some covered with cowhides used as rugs. Very few homes had stoves. They used fireplaces to heat their homes and to do their cooking, using dutch ovens. The roofs of these houses were constructed of poles, grass, and wet dirt. Poles or any form of lumber were as scarce as hens' teeth in that country and these settlers would drive miles to get some building material. They'd put up a ridgepole, then poles two feet apart on each side of the ridgepole, thus forming a skeleton for the roof. Then they'd twist tall grass and mud together in rolls, let them dry, then lay these rolls on the poles of the roof. Wet mud was applied on top of these grass rolls, thus covering the entire roof. This would bake hard and keep out the rain and moisture. Most all houses had homemade doors, and small windows recessed in the wall like the stone houses we have today. Due to the thick walls, these houses were cool in summer and warm in winter.

Fuel was very scarce in Kansas and the settlers burned buffalo or cow chips. That's why they were always anxious to get to the bed-grounds of the trail herds going north. I very well recall the pioneer Kansas women coming to our camp with tubs of eggs, which they'd trade for the bed-grounds. They were all good hands with horses and would come driving teams to our camp. They wore long dresses made from striped bed ticking, tied with a cord at the waistline, and wore their hair down their backs. Their shoes were moccasins made of cowhide. Always the ladies were frank, straightforward in appearance, and possessed quiet, serene looks.

They needed the bed-grounds for fuel, but they were honest

and independent, willing to pay for anything they received. Fresh eggs were their legal tender. How fine in character these pioneer people really were, a far cry from today, when everything is kept going on government loans and subsidies.

Once in a while some fellow would put up a kick to ride into a near-by town. Though we could hardly spare a rider and they'd always get drunk and into trouble when they did get to town, a few of them managed to go. Sometimes when we put the cattle on the cars we could spend a few hours in some little cow town at the bars and cafes. These places were all alike, having plenty of saloons, dance halls, a hotel or two, and a blacksmith shop. There were always buckboards and freight wagons and fine saddle horses tied to the hitching rails. We hated to leave all this, but we remained faithful to our promises and broke up when it was time to ride on. We had started out on a trail-herd job, hundreds of miles of it—the greatest adventure a cowboy could ever have.

Sometimes we'd catch sight of other herds, but we'd keep clear of them. There wasn't a man among us who wanted to mix all those brands. We'd be riding and cutting for days if the stock ever tangled on the trail. We were mighty careful to keep clear of each other, and were plenty tired when we'd graze those steers onto the bed-ground. We'd eat at the chuck wagon, then take turns with the night herd. All we asked was a turn at the bedroll and a chance to pull off our boots for a while. If there was a storm brewing, none of us got any sleep. Baker, as a good trail boss, was a sure judge of not only cattle, trails, and weather, but of the men themselves.

When we came to a crossing, Baker would have the lead steers strewn out free-like, so as not to cause a crowding of the herd. There was never a crush of animals in all that long trip north. One night we had a little trouble with a band of mustangs that somehow got separated from their main band, and they kept us worried for fear they would cause a stampede among our steers.

There was a herd of cattle a few hours ahead of us and we were keeping clear of them to avoid mixing the brands, and they were the ones that caused the trouble. We could see the dust of these critters all day, and that night after we had gotten our steers on the bed-ground these damned mustangs came crossing through the cattle at a great rate. They'd run and nicker, then gallop off with a thundering of hoofs in the night's quiet. We worked for hours keeping them off our territory until some of the riders ran them clear out of the country by morning.

Baker always picked good level ground for a bed-ground. Some inexperienced fellow might insist on running stock into some valley, onto a mountainside, or into a deep coulee, thinking perhaps of shelter, but a steer never picks such a place and neither does a good trail foreman.

He insisted that we not camp too close to the herd and that we keep the camp quiet, too, as far as sudden noises were concerned. We could sing, though, if we wanted to, and the more drony and melancholy it sounded, the better, as it seemed to lull the herd. We took the greatest pains each night on that long trail to water every head of those cattle and give them their fill of grass. It was all this that added up to success in the end.

The trail itself, as I've said, was well planned for us. It lay across the tablelands, or mesas, of West Texas and into Kansas, crossed part of the old Santa Fe Trail near Dodge City, then led onward to the North Platte, keeping clear of Ogallala, that big cow town full of fun and trouble for a bunch of cowboys on a trail drive. We skirted the Black Hills and went on into Montana. We varied somewhat in later drives as herd men found it was far better to avoid all towns unless there were stockyards there. At any rate, these shipping places were nearly all at a distance outside the towns themselves.

We unloaded the steers for the last time at Wichita, Kansas, and took them on across Kansas by trail, then across the North

Platte River and the sand hills of Nebraska. On northwest of Deadwood, South Dakota, we traveled for about forty or fifty miles, going by Devils Tower and the Belle Fourche country. Belle Fourche was a cowman's country in the brakes of the Little Missouri where there was an abundance of fine feed.

We were getting excited by this time. No one seemed tired any more. In our minds we were already spending our pay in Miles City, and nothing could dampen our spirits. We were getting mighty tired of looking at those steers, and yet we had come so far together they seemed like old friends.

We came on down Little Cottonwood and at last crossed the Powder River. We were sure happy at the sight of it, and if we hadn't been trailing those two thousand steers and afraid of stampeding them, we'd have shot into the air to celebrate our arrival, for every cowman's slogan was "Powder River or bust." Though we'd been in Montana for several days, no one could really believe it until we had crossed the Powder.

After crossing, we went over to the Broadus holdings, which were in close on the other side. The town of Broadus was established here on the old site of this ranch. We crossed the Little Powder at the Half Circle Cross Ranch, then went down the Mizpah and on to Miles City. We were now nearing the end of our long trail and coming to the beautiful Yellowstone River. We had practically the same bunch of men we had started with from Mexico with the exception of cooks, for we had had about five different cooks since starting. They would begin drinking at stops along the way and the boss would fire one and hire another. We swam the herd and remuda across the Yellowstone while the wagons were ferried across, and our job was done. The steers were sold to different parties, some to a Mr. B. K. Holt, some to the Bow and Arrow outfit, and some to several others whom I cannot recall.

We were wild to have our freedom, and now, at last, we were

one happy bunch of cowpunchers when Broadus and Hysham paid us off. Miles City was a wide-open town if I ever saw one, but cleaner than El Paso, and without such fights. We had plenty to drink, for there were many saloons, beer halls, and dance halls with girls. Our money melted like snow in the sun. There were some of the finest people living there in Miles City I ever saw. At Fort Keogh there were the cavalry troops with the finest horses, for around Miles was a great horse country. In fact, this little Montana town was the largest horse market of its kind in the world at that time.

Bill Nort, Tom Cottrell, and myself stayed in Montana. I never saw our old cook again, but heard he got a job in a restaurant in Miles City. The other hands went various ways. We had reached Miles City on July 4, 1897, and I was approaching the end of my twentieth year.

Tom and I were eager to get a job and we hired out to an old rancher on Pumpkin Creek, near Miles City. This job was a short one, lasting only a few days—just long enough to put up some hay and corn. These ranchers had a neighbor who had been a colonel in the United States Army. He had a horse ranch and was breeding thoroughbred racing stock. He was very proud of his horses, and well he could be, for he truly had some fine ones. This colonel got me another job with Ed Holt, who owned a ranch on the south side of Tongue River. Tom secured a job with another rancher.

The job at Holt's lasted two weeks while we hauled hay to the government remount station at Fort Keogh, where the government raised cavalry horses. We had a bucket with a rope attached to it and we would take a load of hay down along the riverbank, pull water out of the river with the bucket, and pour the water on the hay. After this we would load on some rocks, then drive to the scales and weigh that water-soaked hay, the rocks, and ourselves, all as hay, and Uncle Sam paid for it. They say that they built a large stone barn at Fort Keogh with the rocks that ranchers hauled in there with the hay. I just couldn't see how these Yankees could be so dishonest, but it looks like everybody wants to cheat their government.

Holt then got me a job with the Bow and Arrow outfit. Ingersoll was the owner, and he lived in Miles City. His foreman lived on Pumpkin Creek. I was put to work on their roundup wagon, and Mr. Holt said he doubted if I could hold the job because he was afraid I couldn't ride those large bucking horses they had. I told him that if I could get up on one of them he wouldn't throw me off, for they were too big and clumsy for any action. They sure could buck hard and could jar you to pieces when they hit the ground, but they couldn't turn, and never would have made a cutting horse. These horses were so tall that when I wanted to get on, I'd take the horse down in some low spot and cheek him. That means I would gather up my bridle reins, grab the bridle, and pull his head around so he couldn't run. Doing this with my left hand, I'd put my foot in the stirrup, grab the saddle horn with my right hand, and swing up. I only weighed about 120 pounds.

We brought in one herd of beef to ship out of Miles City. Some of the horses got away from the roundup, going back to the Pumpkin Creek Ranch. I'd roped a big gelding in the rope corral, saddled him, and led him out to a low spot so that I could get on him to go back after these horses. As soon as I hit the saddle, he lit to bucking. While I was saddling this ornery cayuse I'd noticed two fellows in a buckboard watching me. When the horse quit bucking I'd lost my big Mexican sombrero. I crawled off, recovered it, took the horse to another low spot, and got on him. The old fellow in the buckboard waved to me to come over to where he was.

"Can you kick out a little horse like you can a big one?" he asked.

"Show me one I can't kick out," I replied.

"Come and work for me," he said.

"What outfit do you have?" I asked.

"The Montana Cattle Company, also known as the 79, with ranch holdings in many places in Montana. My name is John T. Murphy and this is my son Bill Murphy," he answered.

I told him I had an idea I would like to work for him, but said I had no way to move my bed at the wagon, since I had no pack horse. He told me to go settle up with the foreman and he would come get me. He called me Kickin' Bob because I was kickin' the frost out of that horse, and to this day that is what all my old friends call me.

CHAPTER VIII

The 79

MR. MURPHY was a highly successful businessman and banker when he saw the possibilities of the cattle business. He entered this phase of business in 1879 and used the number 79 for his brand. He was born in Missouri in 1842, and in young manhood served as a clerk of a general-merchandise firm in Colorado. After a few years of this he decided to go into business for himself and hauled a wagon train of goods to Virginia City, Montana Territory, in 1864 and set up a store to meet the needs of a frontier settlement.

His store was successful from the beginning, so much so that he shipped great loads of merchandise by river boat up the Missouri to Fort Benton and then to Helena, where he had moved his store. As his business grew he began both retailing and wholesaling, as well as entering the freighting business and, later, the hardware business and banking business. He entered the cattle business early enough to secure many acres of range and in later years fed so many cowboys that supplies had to be shipped by the trainload.

On this day I first met him, he took me out to his roundup camp on Sunday Creek, where they also had large shearing sheds under which to shear their many bands of sheep. Here I met Matt Rourke, one of Murphy's wagon bosses of the 79. Murphy informed me that I was to work with Matt's wagon and he was now my boss.

We gathered a large herd of beef and were out on the range

about three weeks at this particular time. The beef was shipped from Miles City, then we returned to camp on Sunday Creek. Here we found the 79 sheep outfit very busy shearing, quite an operation for such a large outfit.

Peg Mendenhall was the manager of the 79 sheep division. He was a top sheep man, versed in all the many phases of sheep raising. He could also get along well with the herders and others who worked with the sheep.

We were all in camp one evening after our return from shipping beef when Bill Murphy came to the roundup camp, asking if some one of us cowhands would volunteer to herd a bunch of wethers until he could bring another herder out from Miles City since one of the herders had quit. No one seemed to want the job, for a cowhand despised to work with sheep, so I asked Bill if he thought I could handle the job. "Yes, I believe you could," he replied, "with the help of a dog."

He took me out to the sheep camp, and if any of you know wethers, you'll know I had my hands full and then some, for they are always on the move, and to make things worse, the dog deserted me at once because he missed his other master. But I stayed with the restless wethers for about ten days until Bill brought out another herder and I was freed of my responsibility as a sheepherder. Bill then brought me back to the roundup wagon, and I took up my work again: bringing in another herd of beef to ship from Miles City.

Bill Murphy then sent me to the LU wagon to work as a rep for the Murphy interests. I repped with them until all the beef was gathered and shipped from Custer, a town in southeastern Montana, located on the Yellowstone and Big Horn rivers, the town being named in honor of General Custer.

One day I was cutting cattle out of a corral when one of the Murphy managers, a man I hadn't met before, said to me: "You

come out to the Big Coulee Ranch this fall and work for me."
Mr. Murphy called me over and asked me what he wanted. I
told him he wanted me to come to the Big Coulee Ranch in the
fall. Mr. Murphy then called the manager over and explained
to him that I worked for him, except when I was with the 79
wagon, and then I was under orders of the wagon boss. He also
told this manager that the reps were sent to the various cow outfits under his direct orders. This manager's name was Tom
Heron. Later he owned what is now known as the Ox-Bow
Ranch on the Missouri River between Great Falls and Helena
in the Wolf Creek area, in the heart of the big-game country.

While with the LU outfit we had a mix-up with the wrong
bed-wagon horses. We had a certain horse broke to pull with the
rest of the horses on bed-wagon duty, a bay with a bald face. The
79 had a horse that was the living image of the bed-wagon horse,
but there was one big difference between the two: the 79 bay
was an outlaw.

All went well until one night we went into Miles and got
liquored up. When we pulled out, it was getting late and the
boss said we were moving the camp out to another place on Sunday Creek. He told us to run in the bed-wagon horses and have
the boys hook them up. I made a rush for the corral, where I
could see the baldface. Thinking all was well, I jumped on him
bareback, like we always did the bed-wagon horses, but I ran into
plenty of trouble because he started bucking like hell. Somehow
I stuck on him and rode him to the bed wagon, where he kept
bucking until I could quiet him down. I was sure surprised, but
being in my woozy condition, I didn't realize just what I
had done.

It was getting dark, but I noticed the boys had hooked up the
bed wagon already. Some of them kept yelling and whooping, so
I got off this horse and listened to what they were trying to say.

The boss of the 79 outfit came up and hit me a crack on the back.

"Hell, Bob," he said, "you rode that outlaw bareback. What do you want? Just name it."

Somewhat dazed, I took a look and thought at first I sure was seeing double, for there were two identical horses, one an outlaw and the other a gentle bed-wagon horse.

I was now twenty-one years of age, and I thought I'd been quite lucky. I hoped I could remain here. But the long northern winters would soon come, and I wasn't sure about a winter's job. These fellows up north had a lot of fun at the expense of us Texans whenever they could get a good joke on us. They thought we were a green bunch of Southerners, and they tried to scare us with their yarns of heavy snows and terribly cold winters, for they knew we were tender to the cold.

At one time there had been a telegraph line into Fort Keogh over a certain route. The tall poles were still standing, though the wires were gone. It had connected the fort with Deadwood, South Dakota. I asked old man Broadus what they were there for, and he said, without even a trace of a smile, that they were the guideline for the stage driver in winter so he could find his way into Miles City. The tops would be sticking out of the deep snow. For a minute he almost caught me on that one, but I recovered just in time, and he roared with that big, good-natured laugh of his.

We were now gathering large herds of cows with calves. The cows were in good condition and the calves were very fat. I had never seen such fat calves before. The 79 had three wagons out on the range doing this work. We brought these herds to the Big Coulee Ranch, where the calves were weaned from the cows. Then we drove the cows back out onto the range. We had three wagon bosses on this job—Ballinger, Titus, and my boss, Matt Rourke. I will always remember Titus because he was such a small fellow, but all cowhand and a good one in any place you might put him.

Every wagon crew consisted of the wagon boss, ten riders, a horse wrangler, and a night-hawk who looked after the saddle horses at night. He drove the bed wagon when we moved camp.

When all the range work was finished in the fall of the year, the entire roundup outfit, consisting of wagon, remudas, and everything used in this huge livestock operation, including riders, headed home to Murphy's headquarters ranch on Big Coulee Creek. This ranch was south of the town of Lavina. Here, like many other ranches I have known, there were long, low sheds in which all the roundup wagons and other equipment were carefully stored until time to be put into use again.

Bill Murphy was the possessor of a very keen memory; he was also very observant and strict about everything to the smallest detail. Sometimes when he went to the various ranches on inspection trips he would take me along for company. We would go from place to place in a buckboard. Bill was a stickler for neatness and planned efficiency. If he walked into a blacksmith shop on one of these ranches, he would immediately miss some tool which was not there or was out of place. The same with ranch kitchens. He would take a sharp look around, miss a frying pan or some cooking utensil from the place where it should hang, and would ask for an accounting of all the missing articles. Much the same with saddle horses and the work stock. When we gathered all the horses to go out on spring roundup, he would crawl up on the top rail of the corral in which we had run the horses, sit there, and take a good long look over all of them. There was always about two hundred head, but if a horse was missing, he would know it. Then he would say: "So-and-so's not here this morning," calling the horse by name.

Nearly all these early-day cowmen were the same, having a

keen value of money and property. You could never say they were stingy or mean about money. They were just conservative, asking for an accounting of the money earned in the cow business. I'm sorry this is no longer the method of management and that so many cow outfits now carry burdens of debt and complain about all the money it takes to run their outfits. *Thrift* and *economy* are two forgotten words in our language, but folks sure better begin to remember them.

The Murphy ranch at Big Coulee had a large two-story house facing east toward the firm's large store, where one could buy most anything. They employed a Chinese cook at the big house. He had a small house for himself out in the back yard, and not only did the cooking, but was also the gardener.

There was also a combination cookhouse and bunkhouse where another cook was employed and where all the hands slept and ate. Then there was a big icehouse where they packed ice in winter for use in summer so they could always have fresh meat and take care of other perishable supplies. This was the first time I had seen ice packed away. They packed it in sawdust. Another old fellow took care of the hogs and chickens, a kind of general chore boy.

Bill Murphy had his office in the big ranch house. Now we were all here at headquarters wondering if we'd be retained or paid off. We'd go over to the office, one following the other, as Bill sent for us. When he had finished business with one hand, he would send for another, until all were accounted for, kept on or turned off. I must have been about the twelfth one to be called to the office.

"Do you have any money?" Bill asked me.

"Yes, sir. I have the wages I've earned." I answered.

"What have you planned on doing this winter?" he asked.

I told him I'd arranged to wash dishes in a restaurant in Miles City for my room and board.

"Would you like to work here at the ranch this winter?" he asked.

I told him I sure would and he hired me for the winter, and I went back to send another hand to his office.

"Did you get let off?" the other fellows asked me.

"No," I replied, "I have a winter job."

"You lucky Texas kid," they said.

I tended sheep camps, herded sheep at various times while herders went off on sprees, and hauled hay to cattle. I didn't stay at the big bunkhouse, for Mike Klein, who looked after the studs and jacks, asked me to stay with him, as he got lonesome out at his house. Mike's place was across Big Coulee Creek, about a quarter-mile south of the big ranch house. He sure loved a nice house with carpets on the floors. He always took his overshoes, or soiled shoes, off on the porch, putting on carpet slippers to wear indoors. He even had a piano, which he could play.

He had been with the 79 crowd twenty-five years when I came there. Two years later he left, going to Lavina, a town on the Musselshell River near the mouth of Big Coulee Creek, and married a lady who ran a restaurant there. He then decided to file on a homestead near the town of Crowd Roundup, which is now a coal-mining town. He always told me every man should own some land. His homestead was also coal land, and he became a coal-mine operator and developed a thriving business at the town named for him, the mining town of Klein.

Among the many persons employed by the 79 were two old Irishmen, Mike and Pat. All spring and summer they would each drive a freight outfit, hauling supplies to the 79 ranches from Billings and Miles City. They spent the winter months going from one ranch to another, sawing wood with a six-foot crosscut saw, and they never spoke to each other all day.

It all happened because one spring they had an argument when they were getting their supplies ready to pull out to freight for the season. Mike was fond of dried prunes, while Pat liked peaches. Mike had prunes in his grub box and Pat had peaches. When they looked over their supplies before pulling out, they found the fruit changed about in the grub boxes. Each one blamed the other, and they were soon in a heated argument. Bill Murphy overheard their discussion and went over to see what the fuss was about.

"Go and see if trade rats haven't been investigating your supplies," he said. "And anyway, what difference does it make? The 79 buys the peaches and the prunes and you can always get more."

But they were stiff necked and ornery, and neither one would apologize to the other, and so they worked in silence when they were sawing wood. Only the sound of the saw broke the stillness of the wintry days.

The 79 always had bunches of old mares they wanted to dispose of, and so they would have some of us cowhands break these out in teams of work horses and sell them to horse buyers, who shipped them to the Southern states, Arkansas, and Louisiana, where the cotton farmers needed them.

Murphy had a big breaking cart built in Helena. It had low, heavy wheels from old freight wagons and a long, heavy tongue, ironed full length where the doubletrees and neck yoke went. He had a huge fir log buried in the ground and two chains with leg-iron rings attached so that we could tie these old mares up and hitch them to the breaking cart.

Watt McCool was an excellent horsebreaker and was never happier than when he could maul these mares around and go on a wild drive in this breaking cart, and I sure liked this excitement, too. Whenever we had no other work on hand, we were supposed to take a whirl at these old broom-tails.

One morning we hooked up two wild ones. The corral where we worked could be seen from the big ranch house, and the Chinese cook always looked on to see the fun. We would catch these mares and harness them in the chute, and that is where the fun began. There was a squeezer in the chute so they couldn't do too much kicking while we harnessed them, but even then they were plenty salty. We would then drag them out with a saddle horse to this huge fir log buried in the ground, tie them to the rings, and hitch them to the cart, but not without a fight. We would throw the corral gate open before we would start, and lots of times we didn't hit the gate plumb center. One of us would get up in the cart with the lines and we would start off on a run, but we had a trip-rope on them so we could pull them down if they got too far out of hand. The fellow left on the ground would have to catch up with the cart and jump in the back end on the run.

Those old mares took off across a big pasture and headed straight for a big washout. When we hit this, we both fell out on our backs. The mares were still on a run with the cart, and all we could do was laugh. The Chinese cook had been watching all these goings on, and he ran over to Mike at the stud barn, yelling that two cowboys were surely killed. We went down and got the old mares when they stopped running from exhaustion and brought them back to the corral.

Sometimes when we had a few hours' spare time we would work out some of these teams, but they sure were raw. Different fellows at the ranch would work at this job every winter as a part of their job. We generally broke out a hundred or so of these mares before the horse buyers came in the spring to buy them.

CHAPTER IX

Repping for the 79

Soldiers and cowboys never could get along and were always quarreling. There were two or three companies of soldiers stationed at Miles City, and once we cowboys were in town loading out beef when a big fight started between us and the soldiers. There was a crowd of both in one of the sporting houses when the cowboys decided they would run the soldiers out. Two cowboys stood at the door knocking the soldiers down as fast as they came out. They beat up one soldier pretty bad. There were two or three roundup wagons camped near town, each with a crew of from twelve to fourteen hands. The Murphy wagon was there, camped on Sunday Creek.

Sometimes we had a hell of a time gathering up the bunch of cowhands when we were ready to leave town, but we were loyal and no one was ever left behind to be ganged up on by the soldiers. When the 79 outfit went back to the wagon on this occasion to pull out for the range again, we found a cowhand named Dobber missing. Matt Rourke sent me back into Miles to see if I could find him. I looked all over town, the jail, all the saloons, sporting houses, and every place I thought he could be, but I just couldn't find him. No one seemed to have seen him after this wild fight. I was beginning to worry about him. I had left my horse at Baldy's Livery Stable while I was looking for this missing cowhand; his horse was in there too.

It was getting dark when I went back to the livery stable a second time to see if he had taken his horse. It was still there.

"Look in all the stalls. Maybe he's asleep in one of them," said Baldy when I went back, ready to give up. Grabbing a lantern, I walked up and down looking in all the stalls and feedboxes and over into the carriage end of the stable. I searched under everything.

They kept a horse-drawn hearse at the stable, and when I was walking around looking everywhere, I saw a hand sticking up next to the glass in the hearse. There he was, asleep, and I went over and waked him.

"Do you know where you are?" I asked him.

"No," he answered sleepily.

"Sit up and take a look around," I said.

His head wasn't very clear after all his drinking, but he did finally realize he was in a hearse.

"I'm sure gettin' out of this vehicle in a hurry," he yelled.

Another Murphy cowhand was Bearcat Williams. We were staying at one of the Murphy outlying ranches looking after cattle, keeping up fences, and doing some wolfing. One day we found a wolf den up against a hillside. Bearcat said one of us should crawl down into the den. He was too big to get down the hole, so I said I'd go, as I was smaller. I started into the hole with a six-shooter, then Bearcat called me back to say: "Don't get excited and shoot back, for I'll be settin' at the entrance with a big club to hit her with if she gets by you."

I'd crawled about forty feet when I came upon a short turn, and there she and her litter of pups were, right in front of me. Her eyes were like two huge balls of fire, and all I had for light was a candle. I shot her right between the eyes, and I could smell blood and feel the trickle of it on my hand. I crawled back out as fast as I could to tell Bearcat that I'd shot her. When I reached the mouth of the hole, he began talking to me, but I couldn't hear a word he said.

The explosion of the gun had deafened me, but he motioned

for me to go back into the den. I still had the six-shooter in my hand, and went back and dragged the old one out. Then I went back several times for the seven pups, which Bearcat killed with a club as fast as I dragged them out. After scalping the wolves we went back to the ranch with our loot. Bill Murphy happened to be there when we went in, and he took us both to Billings, me for an ear specialist and Bearcat to the courthouse to collect our bounty. From Billings, Bill took me to Helena to another ear specialist where I stayed at Murphy's town home until my hearing returned. Bearcat collected the bounty, blew in all the money, and wound up broke, staying with the Salvation Army at Billings. He came back to the Big Coulee Ranch after a two-week spree, but it was well over a year before I could hear well again.

One time we were swimming a herd across the Yellowstone at Miles City. The river was high and swift, and another cowhand and myself were working close together midstream with the cattle. A number of people were on the bank watching us. The young cowhand working with me was from Missouri. He was a little distance in front of me when his horse hit an air pocket, and all the folks on the bank began yelling. I'd seen him there ahead of me; I looked again and he was gone. Then I hit the hole. I was riding a good strong swimmer named Antelope. For those who have never known the thrill of riding a good swimming horse in surging water, they cannot fully understand how much I loved it. You see, the horse and rider are almost one, for the rider gives the horse confidence and he swims well, but all horses are not good swimmers any more than people are.

When I hit the hole, Antelope went down. There was a big black steer right in front of him. I left Antelope in a hurry and grabbed the steer by the tail. This frightened the steer and he swam to shore, taking me with him. As I looked back, Antelope came up again and started swimming. When we hit the bank, I released the steer's tail and scrambled to safety.

76

We found the cowhand's body about a quarter-mile downstream. He had been working to pay off a four-hundred-dollar mortgage on his parents' farm in Missouri. He had a roll of money on his person when we found him. The wagon boss sent the money to his parents, and all of us put in money for his burial and the shipment of his body to his people.

Billy Buck was wagon boss for the Circle outfit, owned by the Conrads, an early Montana banking family who had come to Montana from their large plantation in Virginia to engage in the cattle business. Their family home was in Helena. Art Conrad was one of my dearest friends and was helpful in getting me a job with the Livestock Board later. The town of Conrad, north of Great Falls, is named in honor of this family.

Jack Harris of Highwood, another good friend long since passed away, was general manager for the Conrad ranching interests. Jack came from Missouri when a young boy, his family settling at Virginia City, a very early Montana town northeast of Dillon. Jack told his mother he was going to look for a job and soon succeeded in getting one with a very clever, good-looking dark man herding saddle horses. He was trying to be helpful as a working member of his family but this was not to last very long, for his pleasant employer was none other than Henry Plummer, the noted road agent. He came home one morning and told his mother that Plummer had been hanged to a tree near Helena. It was then he learned that he had been working for the outlaws.

He loved to tell the story on himself when he was working with the Circle roundup wagon. The wagon was supposed to be camped on Dugout Creek, north of Fort Benton, and he went there to meet it. When a big snowstorm hit, he decided to unhitch his team from his buckboard, take his bed, and camp down in a coulee near this creek. Something prompted him to light a match, and there sitting beside him was a frozen man, one of

J. B. Long's sheepherders. It didn't take Jack long to decide that this coulee wasn't big enough for the both of them, so gathering up his belongings, he made haste back to the buckboard.

The first house built in Helena was a log one, now very, very old and treasured as a landmark, and watched over by a care-taker, for there are many Western relics kept there. In 1923, I spent the winter in Helena employed as a doorkeeper in the state senate. One day a party of us decided to pay it a visit, and there I saw a very handsome picture of Henry Plummer. The care-taker asked who it was. No one else seemed to know who he was either. I told them it was Henry Plummer and I knew because Jack Harris, who had once worked for Plummer, had a picture much the same hanging in his ranch office. The tree upon which Plummer was hanged has almost been chopped and whittled away by souvenir hunters.

Clark, the famous wood carver who lived at Glacier National Park, was born on a ranch on Highwood Creek. About twenty-five years ago part of the old Clark home was still intact. Clark's mother was a fullblooded Indian woman. His father, I've been told, was Irish. One time this little boy was very, very ill with a high fever. Everyone said it was typhoid and Jack's father, Harrell Harris, and Clark's father bathed him in a tub of ice water. The shock was so great that it made him deaf and dumb.

Red Bucklin was a squawman who lived where the younger Harrell Harris now lives. Red was an early-day cowman in this section. He built a big two-story frame house for his family. The squaw and the family lived in the new house, but "Old Red" lived by the roadside in an old cabin with a dirt floor. Jack Harris and I went by his shack the day after Christmas one year.

"Red, how'd you spend Christmas?" we asked.

"Pretty tough," he answered. "I bought my wife a half-gallon of whiskey and a carving set. She drank the whiskey and then ran me off with the carving knife."

78

In the spring of 1901, Murphy sent me into Canada to rep for the 79. I was also to represent the entire state of Montana's livestock interests. During my stay in Canada as a rep, though I was still a young fellow, I was serious about my work and wished to do my very best for those who had helped me get this better job. For those who had considered me trustworthy enough for the job, I sat in my roundup tipi in the evenings and studied all the Montana brands in the brand book.

One day two Canadians cut out a cow with a big unbranded yearling following her and started away with the yearling.

"What brand are you putting on that critter?" I asked.

They said they didn't know but the cow belonged to one of their neighbors farther north in Canada.

"No, she don't," I answered. "That cow belongs in the States. These animals belong to the F's run by a wealthy woman in Helena. The Florence outfit on the Sun River runs her cattle for her."

The lady was known to all the stockmen and cowhands as Queen Annette. Her brand was two-pole pumpkin on the left ribs. I then roped the yearling in question, dragged it to the fire, and made ready to brand it.

"What's the brand?" asked the brander.

"Two-pole pumpkin," I answered.

"I can't make that brand," he said.

I took a quarter-circle iron, ran two bars from each point, joined at the lower end, and put the two bars across this.

After my return from Canada, Mr. Murphy wanted me to go back to his Big Coulee Ranch to work with the wagon to ship cattle from Junction. He then told me to take about three hundred head of steers, two-year-olds, farther north in Montana, to what was known as the Northwestern Ranch. Titus, Watt McCool, Matt Gunnison, a cook called Sourdough, and myself comprised the party. When we reached Arrow Creek, we were met by a hand from the Northwestern Ranch with a letter telling Watt McCool to return to Big Coulee. This fellow, John Yuill, helped us to the ranch, taking Watt's place.

Murphy's Northwestern Ranch was located on Shonkin Creek, which heads in the Highwood Mountains and empties into the Missouri River below Fort Benton in Chouteau County. This was in the fall of 1902. When we reached the ranch, Woodcock came out wearing a derby. I asked him to take a count of the steers. He said he couldn't count cattle well, had much more experience counting sheep, so he told me to count out the steers. Woody, as we called him, is still living, making his home in Great Falls. He was the Northwestern foreman. They were short of feed at the ranch that fall and so they couldn't winter the steers.

I found Ben Mandesville, a French Canadian, who had a small ranch up in the Highwood Mountains. He said he'd winter the steers and that it would help him out very much from a financial standpoint. He didn't have any hay, but worlds of straw, as he had threshed a big crop of oats, and there was wonderful grass in the hills. All this was free outside range in those days. He took excellent care of the steers, charged two dollars per head, and rode to keep them from straying away. In after years this fellow built up a good-sized cow outfit, leaving a large estate when he passed away.

Next I went to the Barb Wire roundup, taking my saddle horses with me. Ed Kelly, who was always one of my closest friends, was the roundup foreman. We worked all over the country from Loma, on the Marias River, across the Teton River as far as the old stage station west of Great Falls, then back across the Marias, forty or fifty miles north of the Canadian border at times. I worked here until late in the fall when the roundup wagon pulled in. This was in the fall of 1902. The roundup had thrown all the Murphy cattle across the river near

Brady. These were cattle Murphy had bought with the North-western Ranch from Greenleaf and Patterson, former owners. Brady is northwest of Fort Benton, being named for two early day Great Falls professional men, brothers, one a doctor, the other a lawyer. Both had ranching interests in this section.

There was no feed where they turned the cattle loose on the range, so I gathered all the Murphy animals and brought them back to the Northwestern Ranch at Shonkin. Ed Kelly and I rode all winter gathering up cattle. He had a cattle ranch on the Teton River in a bend of the river known as The Elbow. His boys still own this ranch. Everyone far and near had happy times at Kelly's and Embelton's, as both families were very hospitable.

During the years when I was repping for the 79 outfit on the Crow Reservation in southern Montana, many amusing incidents occurred which I am fond of recalling.

There was the time when Murphy bought the 3V cattle from Mr. Baumanizer, who ran thousands of cattle on his lease from the Crow Reservation. The Murphy wagon had gathered most of these 3V cattle, then Mr. Murphy sent me as a rep to the reservation to gather those we had missed and to stay with the Indian roundup wagon. The government required Baumanizer to work a certain per cent of the Indians on the reservation. These Indian riders would line up side by side and go out on circle to gather cattle every morning. There were ten or twelve of them. A cow-hand called Red Jack worked for Baumanizer. He always carried a bottle of hokey-pokey,[1] and was always full of devilish tricks. He would drop hokey-pokey on the Indians' horses, causing them to run and buck, throwing some of the Indians and causing all sorts of trouble.

Mr. Baumanizer had a government contract to furnish beef for the reservation Indians. About every ten days or two weeks,

[1] Carbon disulphide, or "high-life," which, when put on an animal, drives it into a frenzy.

we would weigh out cattle for Indian beef at the Crow Agency. They had a big buckskin steer they used to lead the cattle into the corral, where they had a scale. All the cowboys would get on the scale too. One day when I first came to the reservation, I was standing off to one side when Mr. Baumanizer said to me: "What's wrong with you? Get on the scale with those other cowhands." So I weighed out as Indian beef every two weeks.

Once we were camped on Sunday Creek near Miles City for the spring roundup when we had an awful spill with the wagons. All the teams were hooked up to the bed and mess wagons when Jesse Coates got up on the RL wagon, intending to watch the wagon men hook up the teams, and was already handling the wheeler's lines. About this time my horse, which I called Bulldog Pup, began to buck, and just as they brought up a lead team for this wagon, there was one hell of a stampede. My pony sure spilled Jess off the wagon, and there was a terrible mix-up of horses, lines, and harness, all the time Jess yelling at me and cussin' me out. I cleared out of there quick and kept clear of that wagon cook for some time.

Another time I remember we had great sport racing the mess wagons there on Sunday Creek. This was all bald, open-prairie country and just wonderful for racing both the saddle horses and the vehicles. Our cook was old Vinegar Jim, and he was about the best cook the 79 ever had.

I'd like to explain here that the wagon worked four horses. It had poles fixed on behind to carry the stove, this latter article fixed securely with rawhide and chained on so that one of these poles came up over the stove's top and one behind it. Two big hooks bolted it to the mess wagon. In addition to these measures, strong ropes were used to keep the stove from moving at all.

In this mess wagon a box held all the tinware dishes, pots, pans, and the knives, forks, and spoons. Old Vinegar Jim acquired this name from making his vinegar pies, which tasted a good deal like lemon pies. I guess you'd call them "mock lemon" today, but they sure tasted wonderful to us cowboys.

This race we planned was to be made from camp to the water hole, some distance away. Jim was an old hand with teams, as he had driven for years down in the Yellowstone Park. He was very tall, well over six feet, and rather on the lean side, but you should see him drive. He could sure handle the ribbons.

The race started, and it wasn't long until the 79 mess wagon lost that stove in the terrific pace. "Have the bed wagon bring on the stove," yelled Jim as he continued to whip his teams. "As long as these cayuses stay on their feet, I'll be the first to the water hole."

He won that race, but when the bed-wagon driver came in, he reported that the stove couldn't be fixed. Then all hell broke loose. Of course they had to go back a distance for it and had to unload the bed wagon. When Jim went back for that "damned stove," he declared it was the roughest three miles he ever jolted over, though it was the same country he had just raced over.

Another time when we camped on Sunday Creek a terrible stampede took place. It was the CK beef herd and we had just bedded them down for the night. The prairie was thickly covered with sagebrush, and out of this came one very small animal which caused one of the worst stampedes I can remember. We had a terrible night, and the dust and confusion were awful. Some of our riders got hurt, but luckily no one was killed, though it was morning before we got things settled down. All this because of one little skunk.

CHAPTER X

Some Cooks I Have Known

I MUST TELL you about some cooks I've known while working for the 79. Bilious Bill was one of them. He was cooking for the LU when I repped there for the 79. I remember it was in the spring of 1903 when we were on Sunday Creek that an old mule played us a dirty trick. The weather was fine and we had worked the surrounding country until we came to the Big Dry where the town of Jordan now stands. We were camped at what the fellows called Lone Tree.

This outfit had an old mule which used to be worked on the mess wagon but was now on the retired list. But come what may, he'd still follow the outfit faithfully. From dawn till dark, from range to range, there he was, trailing close behind.

A number of outfits were camped near by, among them the 79. The cook for this outfit was the one named Vinegar Jim whom I've just mentioned. Jim always tried to have pies for the boys at every supper. Now at this time it was the finest spring weather anyone could want, and Vinegar Jim decided to take the back flap off the mess tent. He had baked some fine pumpkin pies and thoughtlessly left them on the table. Strolling over to where his friend Bilious Bill was sitting in the shade, he sat down beside him to exchange yarns and comment upon the weather.

Just as Jim glanced up from rolling a cigarette he let out a string of cuss words that'd sizzle bacon. The lounging punchers jerked to attention only to see this old mule sauntering toward the two cooks. Jim and Bill were both on their feet, too, and the war was on, for the old mule had pumpkin pie smeared all over his face.

Needless to say, the two old fellows were sworn enemies thereafter. All the boys laughed and joked and tried to get them in a good humor again, but old Bill became even more bilious and Jim developed an even more vinegary disposition.

Bilious Bill got his name from forever taking soda for his "bilious stomach." One hot summer day the outfit had just butchered a beef and left the remains—paunch, etc.—near the wagon. Bill had a very spirited horse which he called Rocky Mountain Boy. On this particular day he was out riding this animal, whose favorite trick was to shy and buck his rider off.

When Bill came to the wagon to start supper, his horse shied at the beef paunch and off went Bill with the first buck. His head hit the paunch, and he got up plenty mad. "Why in hell can't you butcher someplace besides this mess wagon?" he yelled. The fellows claimed he was so bilious after this experience that he could hardly cook a thing for days.

Bill was very fond of cats. He had a big yellow one and had trained him from a kitten to ride with him in a box on the chuck wagon. He was one of the smartest cats I ever saw. When we started to break camp, he would climb on the seat and get into his little box. Here he would wait for the moving wagon. Upon our arrival at a new camp, he promptly climbed down again and watched Bill as he prepared his meal.

There was one thing that this cat seemed to like better than any other, and that was raw doughnut dough. When Bill would cut his doughnut dough, he would pitch the centers to the cat. One afternoon I watched this until I thought surely that cat would kick the bucket that night. But next morning he was there, big as life, stuffing himself with warmed-up doughnuts. He sure must have had the nine lives which cats are supposed to have or he couldn't have digested all those sinkers. In the winter he always stayed at one of the line-camps, and he was a lucky old cat, for he always had plenty of good beefsteak.

I recall the incident of the French cook and the rattlesnake. I was repping for the 79 at the CK wagon. At that time we were near the Canadian border and around Malta. The CK outfit was the famous Conrad Kohrs spread of which we have heard a great deal in later years. Mr. Kohrs's wife seemed fond of bringing over French cooks from the old country and training them to cook for her, or for the wagons. She tried to train them to speak English and understand American ways.

One day Conrad brought out a great big fellow named Joe. He seemed amazed at the mess-wagon setup and could understand very little English. Supper passed without incident, as our regular cook hadn't left yet. Next morning we eyed the departing cook with misgivings, for somehow the boys seemed to know we were in for some bad cooking.

A fellow by the name of Webb was running the wagon at this time and he and I were just coming in from circle that morning. When we approached the wagon, we could hear Joe threatening someone in broken English. There he stood, over six feet tall, with a chef's cap on his head and wearing a long, white apron that reached his feet. Every once in a while he would back up and down, brandishing a long butcher knife at the big bread box.

"What's wrong, Joe?" yelled Webb as we both dismounted and ran toward the cook. We felt sure he must have been taking too much of the bottle.

There was terror in his face as he shook his fist and cried out: "Buzz—eee, says I. Son-of-a-beech, talk I. Buzz—eee. He son-of-a-beech."

I jumped forward and kicked over the bread box and one of the biggest rattlers I ever saw crawled out. Webb's gun took care of him, but the French cook was so scared he had to have us stay around most of the day looking for more "buzz—eees." He wouldn't use that box again, and one of the boys had to build a rattler-proof box for him and put a padlock on it.

He was never any good as a wagon cook, though some of his dishes were tasty enough. Mrs. Kohrs sent him back to France, but we always laughed when we thought of the stories he must have told the people over there. Maybe they believed him, or maybe they thought he was crazy. At any rate, he took chances of being called the biggest liar in town.

Dirty Dave earned this title, not because he was really dirty, but because he was so particular about the washing of the dishes, the dishcloths, and towels. As one cowhand said: "He's plumb soap-and-water crazy, so damn clean that he's dirty." And from this he got his name. His real name was Dave Rankin. He often quit cooking and drove stage just for a change. Sometimes the chuck-wagon jobs got him down because he was very particular about the supplies allowed him and the utensils and other gear used at the wagon. He was the brother-in-law of the famous Pat O'Hara (mayor, saloonkeeper, and supply merchant of Old Geyser in its roaring days), so he could usually be found playing poker and having a few drinks in Pat's saloon.

One year near the end of the season when the supplies were running low, Dave cooked nothing but great kettles of rice and raisins three times a day for three days. The boys were getting pretty short tempered and threatened to give him a ducking in the creek if he didn't give them a change of diet. This dish is known as spotted pup and it doesn't make a bad pudding when served with cream and sugar, but we were tired of it as a main dish.

Dave was nervous that third night as the boys sat down again to this spotted-pup dish. Sure enough, they raised the devil and told him that if he didn't get out the next morning after breakfast and go to a ranch over the hill and get a change of provender, they'd take care of him good.

87

So Dave left the next morning to see what he could find. He was a good rider and was leading a good pack horse as he approached this ranch house. He saw no sign of life, and after knocking on the door many times he called out, "Is anyone at home?" but got no answer.

A nice flock of chickens were busily scratching in the hen house. Dave had come with the best intentions, but seeing there was no one around and realizing that time was passing and he was a long way from camp, he decided to shoo a few of the fat chickens into the gunny sacks he carried on his saddle. This he did without any trouble and started off toward the milkhouse, or springhouse. No one was there either so he helped himself to a fine can of buttermilk. Here was Heaven! Fresh cream; butter; rich cream-topped sweet milk. He was sampling this and that and didn't hear footsteps approaching. A shadow darkened the open doorway, then something hit him. The lash of a quirt hit him over the back. He dodged back and got a glimpse of his assailant. She was a big red-faced woman wearing men's shoes and a Mother Hubbard nightgown. Ordinarily this would have been a funny sight, but under the circumstances Dave failed to see anything comical. This woman meant business, for she had caught a thief red handed and she meant to punish him.

"Take dat and dot, you [here a lot of cuss words in broken English], you stealer!"

Dave recognized this woman as the Dutchman's wife, the terror of the Judith, and he really wanted to get away. He knew now why the boys had sent him to this ranch: it was all a part of a joke.

Still dodging that quirt, his eyes fell upon a crock of buttermilk. It was his only chance. He hurled it full into the Dutchwoman's face, and she fell into the corner spluttering. Before she could rise, he dashed out the door, mounted his horse, and was gone. He said afterward that he spurred his horse all the way to camp and got there with the chickens bobbing up and down in the gunny sack. He put them on to cook in record time.

The heavenly aroma of chicken soup was filling the air when the boys came in for supper. At this moment they thought only of their stomachs and asked no questions. Later his explanation was that it had been "sent from Heaven." No amount of torture could have dragged the truth from him. Best of all, they were heading back to the home ranch at dawn the next day and nobody would care any more what he cooked. This was his last roundup, for no matter how much anyone begged him, he never again signed on as a wagon cook.

CHAPTER XI

Miles City

Ed Kelly, Jim Vieux, and myself were north of Galata across the Marias River gathering poor cows that had not wintered well. After about twelve hours of riding we had gathered quite a bunch of them and were trying to push them into a pasture for the night. We were doing fine until one old cow fell down. We tailed her up, but she kept keeling over. "Bob," said Jim Vieux, "I'll show her what she needs. I'll get her moving."

Jim was an Indian and full of tricks. He took his sheepskin coat, got down on his hands and knees, and flapped it in front of her face. Suddenly the old cow made a lunge and upended Jim, giving him a terrific bumping. There he lay, with his face looking up to the sky, but the worst of it was, the cow had left a stream of manure all over him—from the tip of his boots to the top of his head. Kelly laughed so hard I thought he'd die for sure, and he kept saying to me: "Ain't that the funniest-looking Injun son-of-a-bitch you ever saw in all your life?"

As I've said before, Miles City cowboys and the soldiers stationed at Fort Keogh never got along together; in fact, they despised each other. At this fort were stationed both white and Negro troops, who upon more than one occasion came into Miles and fought some very bitter battles. As a matter of fact, fighting was expected from both groups.

One spring just before the roundup started, we cowboys went into town to have one last fling before the long season's work began. We were going to make it a sort of farewell, as we knew

we had a long, lonesome job ahead of us. There must have been forty or fifty of us gathered there, and about the same number of white soldiers from the fort.

We were at one of the pleasure palaces run by a big woman called Mollie, and we had started to have a good time, singing, drinking, and dancing with the girls, most of whom had just gotten back to Miles City. They usually spent their winters in Chicago, or some other place more lively than Miles. Lennie, a friend of mine from the 79 outfit, was up dancing with one of the girls, who was really very pretty. He'd been making a big hit with her all evening, and she was now wearing his best Stetson. They were really whooping it up.

One of the soldiers snatched the Stetson off the girl's head and proceeded to stomp on it. This was a signal for the fight to begin, and you can bet it turned out to be a knock-down drag-out affair. Webb, the wagon boss for the CK's, always called his men "the CK Pups," and now he yelled for his boys to go after those brass-buttoned men from the fort. Believe me, those soldiers took an awful beating before they ran and hid under the freight wagons outside. The CK's ran right after them, with Webb cheering them on.

Ambulances from the fort had to come get those soldiers, but we only had a few black eyes and scratches to show for the fight. This cooled us off, however, and we lit out for the spring round-up, where there was plenty of real work for us.

I regret to say that my friend Lennie was later killed over the matter of a stolen beef at Gray Stud Springs, north of Jordan. It was a 79 yearling, and Len had just reported it to a Miles City sheriff and had then gone over to eat his dinner at the Miles City Hotel. As he was coming out, he was shot down by a fellow named Rolls, who was carrying a Winchester for this purpose.

Len was greatly loved by all who knew him, and a great crowd gathered to get Rolls out of jail for a lynching. The lawmen prevented this from taking place, but the killer got a life sentence and was taken to the state prison at Deer Lodge. Some time later, along with several other lifers, he made a break to escape and, using a sharpened case knife, killed the deputy warden, Robertson, and almost succeeded in getting Warden Connelly himself. The warden received a few bad cuts, but this Rolls, an Oklahoma half-breed, died there in prison.

Speaking of Miles City, a group of the older sporting women there decided to start a laundry. Perhaps this was because their charms were fading. At the head of this enterprise was Hattie

Dunn, who was the former owner of the Texas House. These girls were successful in securing some ground along the banks of the Yellowstone River. They cut most of the logs for the building themselves, with the help of some of their friends now and then. They constructed a log building twenty feet wide and thirty feet in length. All the laundry work was done by elbow grease with washboards, tubs, and those old-fashioned heavy irons having an attached handle which necessitated a piece of material, generally padded, over the handle to hold the heat away from one's hands. These irons were all heated on a wood-burning cookstove. The cowboys were their best customers. There were pegs driven along the walls; everyone having laundry done had his name above a peg, with his clothes all thoroughly washed, neatly ironed, and hung upon it.

If some young cowboy happened to be short on cash, he could get credit, but very few ever failed to pay what they owed. The women carried the water in pails from the river, heated it all on cookstoves for the washing, but they dug a trench from the building to the river to empty all the tubs and so forth. People in town began to object to this open ditch, so the women covered it with poles and placed soil over them. If any cowboy was without a job over the winter, they would always see that he had a place there to sleep and eat until the roundup wagons started out again in the spring.

It was at the Crow Reservation that we were holding a herd on the south side of the Yellowstone River, and several other herds were waiting there with us for the cattle cars. Along came two squaws with their papooses on their backs. They asked my help in getting across the river to Junction, where there was an old Indian they wanted to see.

I had never been in one of those bullboats before, so I thought I would like to go over in one just for the fun of it and help these squaws out. Two squaws, two babies, and myself made a good load. The paddles were of willow and the hide of buffalo. After we got into the current the boat got to spinning so much I got awful dizzy and mighty sick at the stomach. The squaws took turns pounding me on the back to help me vomit, as they seemed to think that was the right thing to do.

Finally we landed on the north side of the river, and then we went over to see their friend. All they wanted was some whiskey, but he only had three quarts to let them have. He was just about cleaned out with so many riders coming and going while waiting for the cars to come. We got back across all right, but I enjoyed the trip even less than going over, for this time I was worried for fear we would drown because the squaws were passing the bottle back and forth and were getting careless with the handling of the boat.

To make matters worse, we had a bad stampede that night and lost a lot of cattle. Next day Red Jack and I rode toward the mission looking for strays. This was old St. Xavier Mission, and when we got within about ten miles of it, we found a dead Indian at a creek we had to cross. He lay sprawled near the bank, and near by was a half-empty bottle of whiskey. "Let's get to hell out of here," said Red Jack. He was really scared, and we beat it away from there. However, I knew we had to report this, so we set out for the mission as fast as we could. When we told the priest in charge, he called in a rider and had two more men hook up a small wagon and we set out to show them where we saw the body.

The Indian on horseback spied the unfinished bottle of whiskey and drank it. The other two Indians simply pitched the dead one into the wagon, and off they drove back to the Indian mission. The last glimpse we got of them was the body tossing up and down, and we wondered how many times they would lose it before they got back. The only thing Red Jack regretted was that he didn't have the guts to drink that whiskey himself.

I always had a friendly feeling for the Crows, though there were many bad men among them, but you could say the same thing for the whites. Many Indians were loyal friends. Every summer there on the Crow Reservation they would pitch their wall tents and old-style tipis in a wide circle among the cottonwoods, encampment style. Buffalo, too, at that time were still to be found on the Crow Preserve, north of the Big Horn River on the high plateau.

The Cheyennes were also located near Broadus and Miles City, and were friendly and good to work with when we had occasion to do so. These Indians were always poor and lived under adverse conditions. This was later the Ashland community. The Mission of St. Labre had been founded here in 1882, due to the fact that two nuns with guides came here to this forgotten place from a convent in Miles City. They crossed these streams many times and often in high, treacherous water. In these earlier days the Cheyennes were bloodthirsty and warlike and there was often bloodshed here.

The story of these nuns moving into a ruined cabin with a dirt floor was often told us cowboys by the Indians, as well as the white people, who marveled at their achievement. Even the sturdy and staunch Jesuit fathers abandoned this mission, but two of these brave nuns stayed on, working through those long, hard years until 1897, when a resident priest came to take over and stayed. Later, eight sisters and seven priests came to take charge of a modern mission school. When I went back there to visit in 1950, I noticed their wonderful work in their gardens, shops, and dairy. There in the old cemetery were more than one hundred graves marked from carefully preserved old records that the church had kept.

At certain times of the year when the weather was good, all the Indians would start visiting each other back and forth between the reservations. They would get a pass from their own agent and show it whenever they found it necessary and so pass along on their journey. Of course the older ones could not read nor write, but they were the leaders, or chiefs, and they had all the say. No young buck got his hands on the pass or was given any authority.

Many people took an unfair advantage of this fact, and such white men delighted in making fools of the Indians. Once when we were camped with the N Bar N wagon about thirty-five or forty miles north of Forsyth, a Crow chief rode up and asked for the boss. Oscar Dougherty was the foreman, so he came out to see what the chief wanted of him. It was visiting time, and the chief showed him his pass. On one side of his pass was written: "Keep this old boy and his bunch on the move. Don't feed them as they will clean you out and what they don't eat they will steal."

Oscar turned his back so that the chief couldn't see his face. He was dying to laugh, yet he was sorry for these Crows, and he told them to camp below us and if they didn't molest or stampede the stock, they could stay, hunt, and rest awhile. The chief understood English, but he couldn't read or write it. All this seemed to surprise the chief very much, and he said to Oscar, "Little Ox, you are good." Oscar was ever afterward called Little Ox, and he worked for Tommy Cruse with the N Bar N for years. He was afterward a state stock inspector, and the last I heard, he was stock inspector at Omaha, Nebraska. He wrote to me for a long time and always signed his letters "Little Ox."

The N Bar N was owned by Tommy Cruse, the Irishman who became so wealthy in Montana gold and silver mines. He was a poor immigrant boy who came to America, as many others have, seeking a fuller and more prosperous way of life, yet he did love his native sod. Tommy came to Helena's Last Chance Gulch in the early days of the gold prospectors. He was grubstaked by many who knew and believed in him, but his luck came when a lady who ran a small grocery store staked him again. He told her this would be his last venture. "If I don't make a strike this time, I'll quit," he told her.

He made his way back into the hills with his burro, grubstake, pick, shovel, and bed. This time he discovered rich diggings in Marysville, a claim which became the fabulous Drumlummon, christened thus for his birthplace in Ireland. The first thing he did was to pay the lady grubstaker generously for her kindness to him. In 1882 he sold this mine for $2,500,000 to some English outfit, but kept enough strings attached to develop many more mines, which, in later years, produced more wealth for Tommy.

Gifts from Tommy Cruse and his heirs built the St. Helena Cathedral in Helena, and I saw its cornerstone laid in 1908. In one of its spires is a set of beautiful chimes operated from a keyboard. At that time this was something very unusual, and these were very expensive. The windows in this cathedral came from Munich, Germany, and the entire building was a sight to see.

Tommy always remained a prospector at heart. He owned a large ranch near Lewistown, too, known as the Open A 1 Bar, and here he spent much of his time walking around his property. He seemed to walk as a pastime, deeply interested in irrigation ditches and irrigated bluejoint meadows which provided hay for his stock.

On one occasion Tommy went to his ranch and saw a Chinese cook in the kitchen. He took his manager to task for this. "Where did you get that long-haired Chink?" he asked. "Discharge him at once. Don't you know there are plenty of poor Irish people in the country who need work? When I return to Helena, I'll take him back with me."

Tommy sent to Ireland for one of his young nephews. This boy's name was Jim Lynch. He was given a job as overseer on the Open A 1 Bar, and whenever he saw anyone slack in his work, or hanging around the bunkhouse when they should be working, he'd say: "Come to the office with me. I have a remedy for you." Then he would pay the fellow off and fire him.

All the Cruses were as Irish as Paddy's pig, and had a deep affection for their relatives, always looking out for each other. Before he died, Tommy built a private mausoleum in Helena where all the members of the Cruse family are laid to rest.

CHAPTER XII

Marquis de Mores

THE PEOPLE of Montana well remember some of the failures in the cattle business, such as the Marquis de Mores years ago. He really made a boner of the packing business, as well as the cattle and sheep business. We cowboys once had an unusual experience at his abandoned home.

I like to remember the Marquis as part of an era, as folks say. I cannot think of him without thinking of Teddy Roosevelt too, then a young man at his Elkhorn Ranch and his Chimney Butte Ranch. His brand was the Maltese Cross, and his stock used to range from this area over to the Little Missouri Horse Company's range. This was near the town of Baker, Montana. One summer I went over there to attend the opening of the national park named for Roosevelt. I believe it is the only national park dedicated to a single person. My trip back there was as much a memory tour as anything else, but I found out that the average tourist had no real understanding of the celebration at all.

This park is in the Badlands country. The little town of Medora nestles under the whitish cliffs on the Little Missouri. It was started by this Marquis de Mores in 1883, and he named it after his wife. This is really the gateway to the park. The home of this wealthy Frenchman was a grand establishment, called the Chateau de Mores, and it was the show place of the town just across the river.

The last time I saw this house it looked much like it did in the early days except that now no life stirred, other than the caretakers who look after its thirty or more rooms and protect the premises from vandals and fire hazards. The place now belongs to the North Dakota Historical Society. We took some good pictures of the old surrey near the stables and coach house, and also a lot of pictures of the interior of the chateau and its fine furnishings, which were the same in the days of the Marquis, even to the table service. One could almost feel the presence of its noble owners, who lived in such a grand manner.

The Marquis was born in Paris, France, and his wife was the daughter of Baron von Hoffman, a Wall Street banker. The Marquis built his wife a fine church and named it St. Mary's Church. He knew how to live grandly and was really an artist in his own way, but a very poor businessman. There is a big statue of the Marquis at Medora, and a fine hotel named the Rough Rider Hotel in honor of Teddy Roosevelt.

The Marquis could not have foreseen that in three years his meat-packing plant would be a failure. His ambition was to ship refrigerated meat to Eastern markets without paying freight on 50 per cent waste, which was the usual thing. It is said that this Frenchman invested and lost over a million dollars in his venture.

If he had had a good system of feeding the cattle and sheep, they would have been in prime condition for butchering at all times of the year, but he had no system like this. His system was only useful to his packing plant for three or four months each year. His enemies were also instrumental in ruining him.

Medora was not too far from the Montana town of Glendive, and we cowboys used to ride over there to look around and wonder if the place would ever liven up. We liked to imagine we could own such a spread someday. I remember that a saloon-keeper named White came to Medora one time while we were there fooling around. He had the idea he could set up a fancy place here and get the trade from the near-by cow towns. He wanted to set up a regular pleasure palace, with a big bar and

A group of hard-working, fun-loving Montana cowboys. Bob Kennon is standing at left between the two men holding rope coils and behind the man wearing the tie.

Bob Kennon takes a turn driving the wagon in the Powder River country.
He is on the first one, looking back and talking to the boys
about the new camp.

dining room, at this chateau. The sheriff was just about to set out for the place when we asked if we could go along and look it over. "Sure," he said, "you boys come along and we'll make a time of it and see if we can sell this White the idea of buying this *white* elephant."

Of course we hoped White could close a deal and liven the place up with such an establishment. On this, our first visit, we were struck dumb. It was so beautiful that one of the boys said it was fit for a king. The whole place had been left just as they had departed from it. The big closets were filled with clothes, such as the Marquis' fancy coats and suits, silk hats, fancy shoes and walking canes, and also the Lady's trinkets, silks, jewelry, and hats. Both of them were great sports and had lots of riding costumes.

In another room we ran into a real temptation. It made our fingers itch to see all those pistols and revolvers. Here, also, the Marquis had a lot of swords and knives in cases. They were of German and French make and he was supposed to be an expert swordsman in some big military school in France. He used to fly a big flag of this school over the chateau. The flagstaff towered high above the house and could be seen for miles.

All this elegant furniture was wrapped in cloth, and the silver service was locked inside the glass-fronted cases. No one in those days ever thought of molesting a family's personal things; but today one couldn't leave a place unguarded even an hour under such circumstances. Mr. White failed to buy the place and he never returned to the Badlands country again.

Late in June we had just finished the big spring roundup for the CK. We had been spending our pay in various ways, but everything was getting monotonous until one of the boys suggested that we take another trip to Medora. As we were in Glendive at the time and the ride was a short one, we rode over to the Badlands town.

There were a lot of stories floating around about the Marquis and why he had quit this rich estate so suddenly. Not only was there scandal and gossip, but worst of all, the most terrifying ghost stories you could imagine. We made up our minds we would stay the night near the old chateau and see if such things were really true. Most of the boys laughed at the idea of ghosts and thought the whole thing a lark, so we bought some bottles of joy and rode over to Medora.

The Marquis was supposed to have left this paradise empire of his in 1886. He left the key to anyone who would make use of the place for a suitable enterprise, and went back to France. He was later killed by natives in Africa they say, but many claimed he was framed by French political enemies who got rid of him for their own purposes. Anyway, he had surely left a swell spread to the owls and bats, the coyotes and wolves of the Badlands, for the stories which had been circulated about the place kept anyone from going near it by now.

The Marquis had been accused of many things, including the murder of some of his enemies, but it was claimed he did it in self-defense and he was freed of the charges. Many fellows in that day went over the hill by the six-gun route.

There was the story of the man with the black hat. He had been murdered by the men from the Chateau de Mores estate while he defended his water rights at a ditch. He always walked along in the shadow of the chateau walls and wore this black sombrero just as he did in life. His uneasy ghost kept looking for someone each night.

Then there was a man who would go with pick and shovel toward the little graveyard on the slope and dig in the night by lantern light. People swore to the truth of this and that they had heard the rattle of the shovel and pick of this ghostly digger as he made a grave there in the rocks and gravel. Some thought perhaps he was getting it ready for the Marquis in case he returned.

But the story in which we were most interested was about the "ghost light," which both cowboys and travelers swore they had actually seen. On some of our rides out there we would round up a few tenderfoots and scare them with these ghost yarns. They had no reason to disbelieve them if it was getting dark or even if it was a moonlight night, for the place was indeed the Devil's stomping grounds.

It was getting late as we rode out of town that afternoon, but we had cooked up a good plot for the night. We bought flasks of whiskey and gave out the information that we were hitting for the CK range and the home ranch and would not be back for a while. We made a show of stocking up good. The saloonkeeper and bartender hated to see us go, for the place was mighty quiet except when the cowmen came in.

When we were a short ways out, we doubled back on the trail and made camp in the rock walls, out of sight of the roads and trails. We took care of the horses and sat down to make some plans. We had to be sure no one would know of our return and play some ghost tricks on us.

It was agreed that we take all the flasks away from the boys and hide them in a cache until we returned later that night. We were all sober and intended that all should stay that way so we would be sure of what we really did see if there were ghosts at the old chateau. The boys were full of jokes and fun, but became quieter as daylight gave way to darkness. Midnight was agreed upon as the ghost-story hour, so we planned to take up our positions about the premises of the departed Marquis in plenty of time before midnight.

None of us had ever minded being in the Badlands country in daylight hours if the gang rode together. It sounds cowardly to tell this, but there was not one among us who would have set foot here in the dark of night about this chateau. As we rode along in daylight it was a deceiving place to trace horses and cattle in, as the colors were really beautiful. On a bright, sunny morning the white streaks looked like white horses, and there were red, black, and pale lavender, deep brown, green, and orange. These are like the colors of the Grand Canyon and the painted deserts of the Southwest, all of wild beauty. The buttes themselves are stark and bare, looking lonely, but in the early spring the deep snow of the long winter left green vegetation behind for a short spring season.

There were about twenty-five of us on this ride, but some got cold feet toward the end and wouldn't leave camp. Of course they swore they were afraid of real bullets instead of ghosts, so we left them behind. The rest of us were full of confidence and got a real thrill out of the prank we were to pull off. We couldn't have done this stunt on a moonlight night because it would have been too dangerous, and besides, we would never have been able to get into the grounds unnoticed by any onlooker about the place, and we didn't want to be scared by some prankster.

Moonlight nights were scary too, for a fellow could see too much, or you might say too little, on account of the shadows cast here and there across the scene. A pal of mine, Tommy West, and I were very careful and we stuck together as we took the side of the chateau which commanded the whole view of it. We didn't want to be with the gang, as they were sure to pull off some mistake. We were determined to see some of these ghosts, and we had guns ready, too, though everybody knows a gun has no effect on a spirit.

Some sat to watch the carriage houses and the stables, some the cemetery hill and other spots connected with these stories. A June rainstorm was working up and thunder rumbled in the distance. It was a hot night with flashes of heat lightning that lit up those scarred and ghostly buttes. It was a sight a fellow would never get used to. Even the ring of a spur or creak of our boots startled us. We were worked up to a terrible pitch, and spoke in whispers as we watched and waited. I had just remarked that it was hell not to be able to roll a cigarette and smoke as we waited when Tommy gasped and choked. He grabbed my arm and we just stood there, petrified with fright.

"Look up there," he said, "toward the top of the chateau—the ghost light. They're goin' to come all right."

It was all he could do to get the words out. I couldn't speak a word, and it would have taken dynamite to have moved me from the spot as I looked at the top of the house, where there was a weird light. It came all of a sudden and burned quietly. It seemed to come down from the heavens and head down toward the flagstaff and into the old chateau itself.

"Bob, for God's sake, do you see that?" asked Tommy.

"Yes," I answered, "let's watch this thing."

As we watched, it fanned out into a sort of brush-shaped light, though you couldn't see it move. We stood there, I don't know how long, before I came to my senses and grabbed Tommy. Our eyes were still glued to the sight, but we made for the horses, all the time staring backwards as we ran. We wanted to get out of there before the "night visitors" to the chateau should make their appearance, for then we would be a goner.

We stumbled around and got on the horses and rode out of that place. Anyone listening would have wondered at the thundering hoofs that tore along the road. Lord, was that an awful sight, and we sure needed those flasks of whiskey right then. We got back to camp breathless and soon the other fellows came in, all trying to talk at once, and those who had been left behind now wanted to go into town again. We had all seen the same thing, and we never slept a wink in camp that night.

We were anxious to get back to Glendive and report what we had seen and to prove that at least one of the ghost stories was true. After that we were popular fellows and got all the drinks we wanted in any bar just to tell that story again and again. It was not until a year later when a Minneapolis newspaperman and his party camped at the chateau that we found an explanation of this light, and it blew up our ghost story. The newspaperman explained that this sort of light was unusual but was sometimes seen during lightning storms on masts of ships and tall trees. It was called St. Elmo's fire and was really an electrical discharge between the atmosphere and the object itself. In our case it was the tall flag pole at the chateau.

Though I was glad to have the matter cleared up, I couldn't entertain the fellows in the bunkhouses with the "Ghost Light of the Chateau" any more. This was the last time I set foot in Medora until one summer a few years ago when I returned for the park opening.

CHAPTER XIII

Around Square Butte

I REMEMBER when we were working for Ma Hamilton on the Judith roundup near Salt Creek. A bunch of us went into Lewistown one night and took a bartender way out into the range country in a hearse. We were pretty drunk already, and this bartender refused to open up the boss's private stock of champagne and other fancy drinks. We had plenty of money and had already left the place a lot of dough, and felt entitled to have everything we wanted. So we took the champagne and the bartender. We were just throwing him out the front door when the hearse passed by. It had been someplace for a funeral and the team seemed pretty tired. The weary driver sat in the seat, but jumped off when one of the boys stuck a gun in his face. He gave up this sad old vehicle in a hurry. By morning the bartender found himself many miles out of town where the boys had driven the outfit for dear life with him tied in the corpse department.

We kept out of Lewistown for months after that, for there was hell a-poppin'. The undertaker swore that if we ever hit town again, he would give us our last ride in that hearse.

We were riding the Teton north of Fort Benton one time and as darkness was coming on we stopped over for the night at a certain ranch run by a fellow whom my partner Ed and I knew. This place was run by a nephew of a friend of ours, and he was married to a very stylish girl from New York. They had fixed the place up pretty swell with carpets, nice furniture—even a piano—and fancy glassware and china. They were swell folks and this girl was a good singer, and she played the piano and sang for us that night. She even had us singing, too. She must have been glad for anybody to ride in and stay for the night. There was no other woman closer than Benton, and you can understand how lonesome she must have been.

Next morning she was up early and set us a swell breakfast, but here we ran into plenty of trouble with those china eggcups she used, for cowpunchers were used to eating just plain skillet-fried eggs. I looked at mine and was waiting to see what Ed would do. He was watching for me to play my hand. We were in a deadlock over those eggs.

She noticed we were not eating and thought we were waiting for her and just showing our good manners, and so she hurried and sat down. She handled those eggs in a flash of an eyelash. Then we got busy and wrestled ours too. I was sure glad when that was over, for we were dying with shame for fear we would show our ignorance. It was a long time before we met again at a dance at Fort Benton. She was just as pretty as ever and danced real fancy-like, but I could handle her dancing a hell of a lot better than I could those china eggcups.

Another pal, Dick, and I were partners on an alarm-clock deal that he remembered for years, and often we met and recalled how we stampeded the herd one night while punching cattle north of Fort Benton. It was a rainy, stormy night and Dick and I were to stand night guard from two to four in the morning. Now in those days we only had the old sulphur matches and were in a fix to see our watches. I thought of a plan so we would be able to get off on time, for we weren't going to let anyone sleep when we should be hitting the hay. If a fellow didn't come to camp and wake his relief, it was his own fault.

We went to the cook's tent and stole his alarm clock. We lit the lantern and set the alarm for four o'clock, then Dick put it in his saddlebag and we rode to the herd.

Circling the cattle—from twelve to fifteen hundred head—for two hours was a good night's work. The rain and wind made the cattle uneasy as we rode around them waiting for our time to quit. Just as I rounded the herd to meet Dick for the last time, the alarm clock went off. His horse started bucking and he started yelling and cursing.

"God-a-mighty! If you'll just stop buckin', I'll shut this damned thing off!"

This was the moment the herd stampeded.

Bill Sullivan and I had a lot of funny experiences on the Shonkin and Square Butte ranches. One day Bill and I decided to go out after the wolves that were getting away with a lot of stock in this area. There was one old she-wolf that was so cunning that none of us could get her, no matter how much we tried. This was a prize worth having because by her tracks we could see she had pups. At that time there was a bounty paid on these critters. I told Bill we would do it my way and told him to listen carefully while

I mapped out a plan for her capture. We tracked her to her den and then gathered a lot of brush and got ready to smoke her out.

"You sit by this hole," I told him.

He sat down, with his rifle ready, and I built up a smoky fire. Out popped the wolf on a bound.

"Shoot," I yelled, but it was too late. That big wolf got away, and Bill was sure mad at me when I told him he was too slow on the trigger.

"Well, I shot, didn't I?" he snapped at me.

"Yep, you did, Bill, but by the time you saw that wolf she was a mile away."

He got the pups, though, so we went home without a total loss. We got the old wolf that fall and had a good celebration in town with the bounty money. The boss paid us extra, so we had a better time than if we had caught them all together.

Mr. Milner kept a Chinese cook at the Square Butte Ranch, and many were the tricks we pulled on him during his stay there. Milner was partial to the raising of fancy chickens and wanted the Chinaman to raise some Bantams. He told him it was a nice way to make some extra money too. Accordingly, Mr. Milner sent a messenger over to the ranch with the Bantam eggs to give the Chinaman. This messenger gave him a good sales talk on how these chickens would turn out and how well he could do with them.

The Chinaman had been fussing around for days with an old setting hen in the barn, so he was told to put his eggs under her and she would raise the Bantam chicks when they hatched. All this was very hard for the cook to understand, but he did everything the man told him. He was proud of his hen.

Behind the barn that day, Bill and I had discovered a hawk's nest with some eggs in it. That night we killed the hawk while off her nest. We handled the eggs with great care and took them to the barn, where we changed them for the Bantam eggs. The Chinaman tended his hen with regular care. At last, just as Bill and I were getting anxious about the outcome of this experiment, the great day arrived.

The cook had just put the noon meal on the table and we were eating like the hungry men we were when up comes the cook back from the barn, where he had gone to attend his hen. He looked like he was fit to die and kept rolling his slant eyes at us as he talked.

"Some of you boys come quick and see awful little chicks. They just look at Tony with big eye."

Everybody was laughing, and Bill and I would sure have choked on our food if we had stayed. We followed the cook, and he was not only disappointed, but scared of these fierce-looking baby hawks.

That night I asked him how the hen was liking the little chicks.

"Mother hen run away into brush," he answered. "China boy kill big-eye chicks."

He never again attempted to raise fancy chickens for the boss. The secret was never told to the boss, though all the boys knew it and passed it on for a good laugh.

In the years before 1897, Fort Benton was the leading shipping point for cattle, but after this time she lost that honor to Big Sandy. This was on the Montana Central Railroad. In my records I notice that Big Sandy leads all the other points, with 485 shipments; Fort Benton, 422; Great Falls, 59; Armington, 47; Cascade, 38; and Craig, 18.

One night we were all at the hotel after a big dance in Sandy. There were so many of us that we were sleeping in the parlor on the floor and draped on the stairs and in the halls, in fact, almost everywhere one could find a place to pull off his boots. A lot of the boys were too tight to know where there was a bed, or anything else. We were all in, and falling asleep was the easiest thing we did. Before we went to sleep, though, there was a lot of stumbling around in the dark, as someone had taken away the parlor hanging lamp and put it in the dance hall earlier.

We had one fellow with us that sure was a lady-killer, and he had gotten himself the fanciest light-brown suit with a white stripe in it. He had cut quite a dash, and was being extra careful how he put away his pants and coat. He was a tall fellow named Long Barney Williams. He struck a match and draped these long pants of his on the bird cage, which was over where I had made my bunk out of some soft pillows. He hung his coat carefully on a chair back. I can see him yet as he hit the hay after loosening his red tie and keeping his shirt on. He was snoring to beat the devil in no time.

We were all deep in slumber when I heard some woman yelling "Fire!" I thought she was being murdered. I jumped up and yelled for the rest to get up, but there was no raising them, so I groped for my pants to get some matches. I could find neither my pants nor the matches. Finally I got hold of them and after stumbling over boots and other gear, I groped toward the door. I thought I could see the fire on the roof, but it was only the light from a kerosene lamp in the kitchen. Being so sleepy, I was confused, and I kept trying to get into my pants, but they seemed to be tangled up. Finally as I was crawling into them in the hallway, a girl came flying down the stairs and kept dragging at me to come up and help get her trunk out before she lost all her belongings.

When I succeeded in dragging these pants on, they came all the way up to my chin. I'd have died before I'd let her see me in that shape, fire or no fire. About this time the boys started joining us, creating a terrible noise with their cursing and yelling. I got out into the street away from that girl, who had started on some of the rest of the boys to help her, and I joined the bucket brigade.

The fire proved to be at the other end of town. As I remember, I believe it was the Marsh Hotel and Swanson's Saloon.

I wasn't much help because these long pants kept slipping down on me, and as soon as I tried to hand up a bucket of water to the fellows on the ladder, I had to reach to pull up my pants. They were tripping me so much I gave up my place and went to the back to see if I could sneak back to our hotel parlor and find my own pants. By now I was beginning to worry about Long Barney finding out about his pants being gone.

Those handsome pants were a sight with water and mud and burned-wood marks on them. I kept thinking, too, of the roll I still had in my own pants, for Long Barney's were plumb empty of jingle. I was just making my retreat when some men saw me and yelled to me to help, as the saloon and barbershop were now on fire and the wind had changed just right to wipe out the whole town.

We fought there until daylight. I stumbled about in these big pants, hoping that Long Barney wouldn't see me in them. Just as we got the fire under control and someone started handing out coffee—and a promise of a big treat at the saloon which we had saved with its big stock of good whiskey—here came Barney. First we stared in terror, for we thought a wild Indian had come in on foot to terrorize the town. He was wrapped up in a bright-red blanket from the hotel, and he was plenty mad.

"Where the hell is the s.o.b. who took my pants?" He was red in the face and cussing so much he could hardly get his breath.

The fellows were all laughing and hollering at him fit to kill, and somebody jumped him from behind, knocking him down and revealing his condition. He had on pants, but they were mine and they didn't reach much below his hips. I came from behind an old wagon where I had been hiding, and told the fellows to let Barney up. They made a rush for me, for I was a sight to behold. Barney joined me, and we held them off with rocks until we could trade pants. We were so glad to be dressed in our own pants again, and now that the fire was out, we headed for that saloon, and the rest of the day in Big Sandy was one big celebration.

The next day we went out to Tingley's and sobered up. In earlier days the Tingleys lost a lot of oxen and horses to Indian thieves. When this estate was settled, the government had to make good these losses to the amount of several thousand dollars. It was a big horse spread and they were very successful in raising really beautiful horses for many years. Their ranch was up in the Bearpaw country.

Ole Osness owned a big sheep ranch near Square Butte, and in the wintertime, anyone who rode into town and was going by Ole's ranch was asked to take his mail out to him. The snow was deep the day I rode in, and Mike Callahan, who ran the store and post office, asked me to take Ole's mail out. "I've got an awful lot of mail here, a two months' accumulation," he said.

When I got ready to leave, I took my horse around and picked up the two seamless sacks of letters and papers. It was a fourteen-mile trip in all this deep snow and was really tough going, for the snow had crusted into high drifts in many places. The two bags of mail had holes cut in them to hang over the saddle horn and thus rode well. As we plunged along in the drifts, I thought how happy the fellows at Ole's would be when I arrived with the mail. It had been two months since the herders had seen a newspaper, a Sears-Roebuck catalog, or a letter from someone far away.

When I arrived, Ole met and thanked me heartily for bringing the mail. He told me to put up my horse and we would have supper soon. When I came in from the barn, Ole was seated on the floor in his little office, and had pulled a big box from behind the stove. He was filling this with all the newspapers I had brought. The letters he was piling separately.

"What the hell you doing?" I asked him in surprise.

He then started burning the papers.

"I can't let these damned Swedes and Norse read these papers," he answered. "They'd get too damned smart. The wages for herders are published here. It would break Yesus Christ to pay them if they read this."

Another day I stopped in to see Ole and found him getting ready for lambing. He had lots of help and all of them were Swedes right from the old country. He needed someone to go to Fort Benton to drive a four-horse team and bring out a big load of grub before they started work.

"By Yee, Bob, I'm in a bad fix," he said to me. "I need a four-horse load of grub here at the ranch before lambing and none of these greenhorn Swedes can drive a four-horse team. Would you do me a favor and go to Fort Benton and bring out the grub?'"

"Ole," I answered, "I'd like to help you, but you know I work for the Murphy outfit."

"I'll clear that up with Murphy," he answered, so I consented.

It was in early April and lots of birds were back again from their winter homes. I noticed a lot of these long-billed curlews in particular as I drove along. I pulled into Power's Store and we loaded the grub for Ole, then I went up to stay at the Overland Hotel for the night.

The next morning I heard from the hotelkeeper that a Swede had arrived from the old country and was expecting someone to take him out to Ole's sheep ranch. He was brought up to my hotel, and when I saw him, I started to shake hands and welcome him to Montana. He didn't move a muscle and seemed to be dumb. Maybe he didn't speak English. He was a big, tall fellow and real young. Not being sociable was almost a crime in this man's country, so I let him sit still there on the high seat as we pulled on the stage road for Square Butte and Ole's ranch.

As we rumbled along for miles the Swede remained speechless. Soon one of those long-billed curlews flew along ahead of us in the road. First the Swede looked mad, then he screamed: "Yesus, what is that?" I was sure surprised at his English, but it was my turn to play dumb so I didn't answer him.

After the twelve-hour ride was finished and we had come to Ole's ranch, the Swede got down off the seat. "Yesus, did he have one helluva bill!" was all he said. Even to this day, every time I see a curlew on my ranch, I think of that greenhorn Swede.

A chuck wagon near the Musselshell River. Note the horses grazing in the distance.

Branding for the WD south of the Musselshell. Bob Kennon, wearing a tall, white hat, is holding the critter's leg.

CHAPTER XIV

Some Pranks

WHEN I was stock inspector, I had to pass on a bunch of horses that were being shipped from Square Butte to the Miles City yards. It so happened that these horses got loose from the riders and got over into the brakes and badlands. We had to ride out and hunt them down and then rope them. We necked a wild one with a gentle one to drive them in. Finally we got them loaded for Miles City and saw them pull out. We were a happy bunch after fighting those jugheads for several days. One of the owners gave me a twenty-dollar bill to treat the fellows.

Two fellows ran a saloon there in Square Butte. They called it Bob and Jack's Place. It wasn't much and had a floor made of two-by-fours with a cellar below in which they stored the jugs and bottles of booze. We got pretty drunk celebrating and I noticed that an old farmer had tied a big work horse outside at the hitchrail. This gave me an idea. I went out, got on this plug, and rode him into the saloon onto those two-by-four floor boards. Bob and Jack were so sore they went after the town marshal. When he came, I was sitting out in the middle of the street. "I'm after you," yelled this marshal when he got within about thirty feet of me.

I fired a shot or two over his head, and he began to run. The faster I shot, the faster he ran for home, and the neighbors said that when he got there he locked himself in. He sent his wife downtown two days later to see if I'd left town. The bartenders told her I'd gone back to Fort Benton. He then very bravely went about town and said he'd arrest me if I ever returned. He made this boast in the presence of a crowd in this same saloon, but some wise guy laughed and said: "If ever you do arrest him, it'll have to be on the run."

One day in the early spring we heard about a big dance being planned down on Highwood Creek. After the long winter, George Jeffries and I felt like going over and making a night of it. The dances in Highwood Valley always were a lot of fun, as the people came from far and near to attend them. They were noted for the wonderful suppers and for the pretty girls. Sometimes a good-looking schoolmarm would cause a big stir and give us the thrill of dancing with her. The word went out that there was to be a prize given the best-looking man and one for the prettiest girl.

We were over on Arrow Creek at the time and it would be a sixty-mile ride into Highwood Valley. We rode hard, but were late, as the music was pouring forth from the open windows and the dancers were having a good time when we got there. The yard was filled with top buggies, wagons, saddle horses, buckboards, and all sorts of ranch vehicles. We were getting off our horses when some friends yelled to us: "Hello, Kickin'! Hurry up! They're goin' to give out the prizes soon!"

We got into the big log hall and found it jammed with people all clapping and laughing. Pretty soon, George, who had sandy-red hair and freckles, was called up by the prettiest gal in the whole room. She presented him with a beautiful cake, all frosted and fixed up fancy. It was his prize, but being so flustered and embarrassed, he laid it back on the table. The rest of the night was spent eating a wonderful chicken supper, with cake and all the fixin's.

The party broke up at daylight, and George got his cake, put it in the box, and we saddled for our trip home. We planned to eat the cake when we got hungry along the road to the Arrow Creek Ranch. It was getting on toward midmorning when we decided to get off the horses at a small creek, water them, and eat some of the cake. Our mouths were just watering as George took the box of cake out of the flour sack in which he had been carrying it behind the cantle of his saddle.

I got out my pocketknife and cut two big slices while George was getting some water from the creek above the saddle horses. As I cut into the cake I found a slip of paper, but paid no attention, just tossing it off on the grass.

George came up, grabbed his piece of cake, and took an enormous bite. He let out a yell, then almost strangled as he gulped down some water.

"God-a-mighty! Taste that cake, Kickin'," he said with his eyes watering and his tongue burning.

I did, and found that the frosting was made with salt instead of sugar. Then I remembered the paper, and picking it up, I read: "First prize for April Fool."

Just then we realized that last night had been the first of April.

Once I was repping for the P Lazy N outfit and we were just about finished with the shipping of the beef at Big Sandy. At this time, over by the stockyards, there were some women's tipis which belonged to a bunch of dames who had come down from Great Falls. We called these gals "tipi gals." They were there to get all the boys' pay, as we were paid off here. Everyone was drunk the night we finished and still celebrating the next day. McNamara and Marlow just about owned the TL outfit and they had a foreman named Sam Miller. A pal of mine named Harry was with me and he was a devil for pranks. We were up to our usual tricks on each other, and just dying to get a good joke on Miller. We watched to see if he would go into one of these tents by the stockyards. We were riding around roping everything in sight when Harry spied old Sam go into one of these tents. They were strongly made, with double doors which could be locked from inside or outside.

"Get your rope, Bob," yelled Harry.

We roped and dragged out this tent, and down the street we went. Now old Sam had no chance to get out those doors, and besides, they were on the ground side.

Ike Rogers was then running a saloon in Sandy, and he came out betting on who was in that tipi. He was followed by a bunch of yelling, whooping cowboys, who were now wilder than Indians. This brought McNamara himself out of his store to see what was going on. When we got down in front of his store, we stopped and took the rope from the tent and old Sam came crawling out just madder than hell. He swore to kill us sure. What made it worse was the fact that this woman came crawling out after him, looking like a porcupine. McNamara's face was purple with rage. "You're fired, you s.o.b.!" he yelled. "You ain't no foreman of mine."

When we got the cattle shipped out, we went back to the P Lazy N. We had a lot of fire-water along with us even when we got to the home ranch. The boys were sure feeling wild and reckless, and were just about ready to pull off any kind of stunt. The ranch house itself was made of rock, and on one of the walls in the dining room hung a big photograph of the owner's former ranch and a big herd of cattle. He prized it highly. He also had another article which he valued very much, an old buffalo gun which always stood in the corner.

It's a coincidence that this old buffalo gun had formerly belonged to John Madden, an uncle of my wife, Marie. This old gun hadn't been fired for years, but was loaded just the same. Unfortunately, I picked it up and pulled the trigger. The bullet took out the picture and a square block of rock from the wall.

After I had done this damage I said I would go see Mr. Norris. Now when you went into his office from the store, you had to step down. I missed the step and went headlong and hit Mr. Norris in the belly with my head. "Drunk again" was all he could say.

Bill Norris was half-owner of a ranch on the Judith River. One time Bill and I were subpoenaed as witnesses in a shooting scrape which took place on the Judith, so we had to take the stagecoach at Claggett to Big Sandy, then go on to Fort Benton the next morning. It was necessary to stay overnight in Big Sandy and we put up at the old Spokane House. This was a two-story log building, and a deathtrap for cowpunchers who came in late or were lit up.

Next morning I got up quite early, long before Bill was astir, and I couldn't for the life of me remember just how I got up to my room the night before. Instead of turning left when I came out of my room, I turned right. Then I saw a door, opened it, and stepped out quickly. Straight down I went, seven or eight feet, landing right in front of the barroom door. It was a wonder I didn't break a leg or so. I gave a bloodcurdling yell when I took off toward the ground. The bartender heard me and came out.

"What the hell you practicin' for? The circus?" he yelled.

When I'd picked myself up and found I was still whole, Bill came running down, tripping over his pants and with his suspenders down.

"Why the devil don't you fix them steps," he raged.

"They been that way for years, and we ain't aimin' to fix any new ones—too damned much work."

I remember an incident which happened down at Suffolk, on the Milwaukee Railroad, where we liked to camp for the spring roundup. The Circle C, the 2 Bar, which was Frank Stevens' outfit, and the 72 Bar—all these brands were represented here. The

P Lazy N had a foreman named Milsap, Horace Brewster was there for the Circle C, Frank Stevens for the 2 Bar, and Hamilton for the 72 Bar.

For three springs in a row a very odd thing had taken place here. Three men, all from the Circle C, had died, one each year, when we had camped here at Dog Creek. One died in his sleep, one was dragged to death by his horse, and one had his neck broken in a fall over a cliff. Brewster was more than a little annoyed and couldn't seem to understand it any more than we could.

We had been coming in all day, the different reps and cowpunchers, but still no Brewster. Along about sundown I saw the Circle C outfit pull in way up on a hill some distance from the rest of us, so I decided to ride up there and ask some questions. Old Horace didn't take kindly to my joking, and got a little huffy when I asked him what he was doing up on this hill. "Hell, Bob," he said, "Coburn ain't aimin' to start no private cemetery down in that coulee."

Brewster was a very superstitious man. He was the man, when foreman of the roundup on the Judith in 1881, who gave Charlie Russell his first job as horse wrangler.

At another time when this same wagon boss, Horace Brewster, was still at the Circle C, we started taking a herd across the Missouri at Rocky Point. It was in the fall of the year and they were to be put over on the north side for the winter range. Then in the spring we would throw the cattle on the south side of the river again.

Coburn, owner of the Circle C, had a breed fellow who spoke only broken French and English and was called Parley Voo by all the boys. If he had any real name I never heard it, but he was a good fellow and helped the cook, did errands, and such. At this particular time, Bill Coburn was with us and was working the cattle not too far from me. I looked back and there crossing with

the steers was this young breed Parley Voo. I tell you I was about
to faint, for he was already up to his waist in water and we were
sure getting into some real swimming water.

I yelled to Bill and pointed to Parley Voo, but Bill couldn't
hear me or see this fellow. Somehow we got that breed across,
but I just knew something awful was happening to him. We got
over and I rode back on the bank of the stream and saw Parley
Voo wringing out his pants and grinning. Bill rode up then, too,
and we gave him the devil for this stunt. "I not drown—I got
the gum boots on," he kept reminding us.

An Indian boy rode with us that day and remembered this incident well. He is now my close neighbor. His name is Jack
Gardipee, and we often sit and relive some of the old range days
of the past. His father was killed in a bear's den, and it worried
him because his father and mother were not buried side by side,
for his mother was buried in the Lewistown cemetery. One day
he dug up his father's bones, put them in a sack, and buried them
beside his mother's grave. "Now they sleep there happy for
always," he said.

CHAPTER XV

Varied Experiences

IN THE SPRING of 1903, I worked on the roundup with
the LU Bar outfit. We were camped at the Coal Bank Springs
north of the Missouri River. This was the spring of the big May
snowstorm. Three of us were ordered to go back to Billings to
throw all the cattle back across the Missouri River. These cowhands were Bearcat Williams, Porcupine Sellers, and myself.
Four trainloads of cattle had pulled into Billings just before the
storm hit. All these steers were from Texas and belonged to the
XIT, the Long X, and the cattle firm of Kirby and Christianson.
The streets and alleys of Billings were lined with dead cattle, as
they had unloaded them from the cars. A bunch of cowhands
from Texas had come north with the cattle, and they had never
seen so much snow at this time of year, even up here in the north.
They stayed in the caboose all the time they possibly could, for
they were almost frozen. You can bet your bottom dollar they
high-tailed it back to Texas as soon as they could.

When the wagon wasn't working the range, the reps had to
work on day herd. When the storm hit, I was out on day herd at
Coal Bank Springs. I didn't have any heavy coat or overshoes,
for it was late in the spring. The snow was sure coming down and
it was getting colder all the time. I happened to see an old
deserted sheep camp and near it was a scarecrow, placed high to
scare the coyotes away. It was a post put into the ground, with a
stick nailed onto it for arms, and was dressed in an old sheep-

lined duck overcoat and a pair of sourdough pants lined with flannel. Inside the camp was a pair of mittens.

"Well," I said to myself, "I need those warm clothes more than that scarecrow and this is sure a piece of good luck." I undressed Mr. Scarecrow, dressed myself up, got back on my horse, and went on with my job, maybe looking like a scarecrow myself, but a lot warmer.

Another bunch of cowboys came out to relieve those on day herd, and this is when they sent a rider to relay the message for us three cowhands to throw the cattle on the north side of the river. We crossed below Rocky Point on the Missouri, and had been able to count dead steers all the way from Billings to Razor Creek.

Next I was sent to the 2 Bar wagon, "Spud" Stevens' outfit. Spud had squatted on a claim near Fort Maginnis, the fort being so near he seized the opportunity of supplying it with potatoes, and this is how he got his nickname. He continued to live in a small sod house, raising his spuds, investing his money in cattle until he succeeded in buying several ranches and building them into successful ventures. Among them was one called the Red Barn. On one occasion El Silverthrone, Frank Stevens, who was Spud's nephew, and myself were at the Red Barn. Spud cut open a paper sack with his jackknife, just an ordinary paper bag like those in a grocery store. He then took a big, heavy pencil and began writing. "Boys," he said, "I'm writing my will."

He left each of his sisters a legacy. Before this he had bought a home for each of them in Lewistown, but he left the major part of his estate to his nephew Frank Stevens. When Spud died and the will was read, Roy Ayers was a judge of the district court in Fergus County. Later he became governor of Montana.

On Spud's ranch were a lot of beautiful peacocks which he raised for pets, and running around also by the dozens were cats,

cats, and more cats, cats of all colors and sizes. These were the pets of a fellow named Whitehead, and he thought a lot of these cats—just loved to see them in the barns and haymows, and at milking time he would often squirt fresh, warm milk into some tabby's mouth. Stevens said the cats had to go, but Whitehead refused, and declared: "If you keep all those peacocks, I'm going to keep my cats." He held out, too, and there was war brewing.

Finally Spud hired a bunch of half-breed boys to round up these cats and kill them on the quiet. He offered them two bits per head. We got wind of it and decided to have a good joke on old Spud. We went to the breeds' camp and told them it was terribly unlucky to kill a cat of any color, and they had nine lives, and would bring them bad luck for seven years after the killing. That night the breeds had a meeting and upped the price to a dollar per head, or they wouldn't do it at all.

When Spud's will was finally read in court, the room was packed to the doors and the crowd was quietly listening to each article as it was read. Then a deathlike pause, and the voice of old Whitehead loudly asked: "Say, who'n hell gets to kill them peacocks?"

One time Spud sent another cowhand with me to work at Rocky Point. This cowhand decided to quit and wanted me to go back to the ranch with him to see Spud. He had borrowed some money from me and wanted to pay it back, so we went back to the Red Barn and found Spud there. He told Spud he would like to quit and go to Seattle, where his people lived and where he could get a job as a streetcar conductor.

"I have some money coming, so let's settle up," he said.

We were all in a big shed. He and Spud argued a few minutes about how much he had coming, then Spud pulled out a chip which had been hewn off one of the logs.

"I've already paid you ten dollars," he said, looking at the record on the chip.

This might be an unique way of keeping books, but that was how he did it.

Another time Spud decided to give a big dance for everyone in the community, as well as for all his friends from Lewistown. One lady asked him where she could find a toilet. "Well, lady," he answered in his typical fashion, "just go out in the sagebrush."

He made so much money in the cattle business he thought it would be quite a business deal to build a big sporting house in Kendall. This was a mining town, an old gold camp northeast of Lewistown in the Moccasin Mountains, and like all old Montana gold camps, it is now a deserted ghost town. Spud and the madam of this house took a trip down south one winter. Incidentally, this house acquired the name of Spud's home ranch. I had told Spud my sister lived in Dallas, Texas, and had asked him to go see her while he was down there. This he did, taking his lady friend along and introducing her to my people as Mrs. Stevens. When they had completed their visit in the Southwest, they traveled on down into Old Mexico. My sister wrote me saying all the family were pleased to have met "the Stevenses" and that Mrs. Stevens was such a dear lady. I kept all my knowledge to myself, but I've often laughed about this because all my folks were such strait-laced Baptists.

I worked at the 2 Bar wagon, repping for the 79 until September and we had shipped out the cattle, then returned to the Shonkin wagon. Cy Buck was the wagon boss, assisted by Joe Doyle. It was very dry on the Shonkin range despite the fact that we had so much moisture in the spring. The ranchers found it necessary to move all the horses and cattle across the Judith River near Rocky Point. Herd after herd were moved onto this range. We were trailing the last herd between Thanksgiving and Christmas. When the tail end of the herd, or drags, as they're called, had crossed the river and come up the hill, I couldn't help but wonder what was holding up the herd so long. I rode back to find out, and when I reached these two drag riders, they were having a hot argument. Both were half-breeds, and had been off their horses and had a fist fight. One boy, Jimmy King, said they were arguing about who was born on Christmas day. "I said I know it was Jesus Christ, but he said it was Moses," he told me. I told them to get back on their horses so we could get the herd up the hill before dark and bed them down.

Jimmy King spent the winter with me in a line-camp once. We lived in a little log cabin with a dirt roof. One day we decided to clean the stovepipe, as it was not drawing well. Jimmy was on top knocking out the pipe with a long pole. He had an old pair of overalls tied on the pole to make a swab. I was inside, ready to pour kerosene on paper, touch a match to it, and burn out all the remaining soot. I asked Jimmy if he was ready for me to touch the match to the paper. He wasn't quite ready, but I misunderstood his reply and touched it off. I went outside to see how Jimmy was doing, and such a sight! His face, eyes, and hair were covered with soot, and his hat had blown off his head. His eyes looked like two holes in a blanket. We started a fire in our new clean stove and heated some water to scrub Jimmy and look after his eyes, which were now in a painful condition.

I spent the next three years in line-camps looking after 79 stuff, as well as that of other outfits, always with a different cowhand as a partner. Red Jeffries stayed with me two years. In our spare time we would make rawhide ropes, quirts, and bridle reins. One time we sent a number of these articles to Al Furstone and Cogshell at Miles City. They must have had a value of at least two hundred dollars, but this outfit sent us a check for only twenty dollars. That is all we had for our hard work.

We lived in tents, with pine boughs on top of the first tent and another tent stretched over the boughs, thus giving added warmth. From one to one and a half feet of snow was on the ground, and we burned wood for fuel in an old government box stove which we got from a fellow at Rocky Point. There was no bottom in this old stove and the top was also missing, but we found a long, wide piece of iron down at Rocky Point and put wood in the top. We had a hole dug under our bed to keep our potatoes, canned corn, and tomatoes in, and slept on them to keep them warm. We had no hay for the horses, just oats and what grass the horses could paw from under the snow. We kept a horse hobbled all the time so we could wrangle the others. We drifted the cattle off the Shonkin range onto the 2 Bar and P Lazy N range.

The last year I spent in a line-camp, Harvey Mitchell, a young man from Indiana, was my partner. He had come to Montana with a carload of horses for Fort Benton. I met him there and he said he would like to get a job with a cow outfit. Harvey was a keen lover of good horses. Abuse a horse and you would have him on your neck. When he said he would like a job, I told him I'd take him out to Murphy's Northwestern Ranch on the Shonkin where he could get one. While Harvey was with the Northwestern Ranch, I bought a bunch of cattle from a colored woman who was cooking for the Turners on the Marias River.

Harvey would often ride range with me while we were both at the Northwestern. There was a big alkali lake on the ranch, and the cattle I'd bought had never had experience with alkali bogs, so six or seven head bogged down in this lake and we had to pull them out. Harvey and I are still close friends. He is in business in the old town of Augusta, about twenty-five miles from my ranch home. We often meet and talk over our range days and he still jokes me about those green cattle getting bogged in the alkali holes.

Ranch owners strongly objected to the cowhands playing poker, for they said we stayed up too late at night and next day couldn't put in a good day's work. So we played a game with a top. We would mark *A P T N* on a little stick sharpened at one end. Everyone put in two bits. When the top stopped on A, you got all the winnings. P meant put in one and T, take out one. N stood for "nothing." On rainy days when we were not working on the range, we took up this form of gambling. I remember one evening we were playing and I had excellent luck, winning all the money, about thirty dollars. I put it in a buckskin sack, keeping it in the jockey box of the mess wagon. Al Wandliss was the roundup cook and was the only one who knew I had it cached in the wagon. I fell asleep under the wagon, and the boys whittled a bunch of shavings and placed them near my hip pocket. I had a pair of buckskin gloves in this pocket which they mistook for the buckskin sack with the money in it, so they set the shavings on fire and this sure woke me up. The fire burned a hole in my hip pocket before old Al, the cook, could pour a bucket of water on me to put the fire out.

Once when I was repping with the P Lazy N wagon, Powers fired a wagon boss named Green who had worked for the outfit for years. He asked me if I would run the wagon until he could hire another wagon boss. He wanted a man from Texas and asked me if I knew any fellow I thought could handle the job. I told him I did and recommended a Texan by the name of Frank Milsap who had worked for the XIT in Texas.

Milsap accepted the job, taking over the roundup wagon. Frank didn't know the range nor understand the Montana method of gathering herds, so he would always ask me to lead the circles. There were four wagons at that time and we had reached the lower end of Powers' range below the mining town of Kendall. The Powers wagon, Shonkin wagon, 2 Bar wagon, and 72 Bar were on this roundup. All the wagons were camped six or seven miles from Kendall, but we rode into town so we could go on a spree.

Milsap always wore a long, sandy-red mustache and always spoke of Montana people as Northern Yankees. I asked the bartender to give me some of the limburger cheese he had. Milsap always put his arms around my neck and told me I was the only one up there in Montana that he cared for, as I was a Texan. I worked the cheese through my fingers and rubbed it into his mustache. He was so drunk he didn't know what I was doing, but when he got a whiff of that cheese, he took his hat off, threw it on the floor, and said: "I can whip the feller who so-and-so'd on me." This was a favorite trick in Montana in those days. Charlie Russell used to play it every chance he got.

After Frank Milsap had been a wagon boss at the P Lazy N for about a year, he sent to Texas for his brother John. I sure loved to play jokes on good old John. He was a roundup cook at the P Lazy N wagon, but he could also play some fast ones and sure did on me. One time I unrolled his bedroll and put some prickly-pear cactus in it. He must have suspicioned me as the fellow who played this trick on him.

Every spring I bought a new slicker. I always kept it on my saddle so I'd have it handy if a heavy rain came. I still led all the circles, dropping off riders here and there so we could pick up all the cattle and drive them to the roundup grounds. When we were branding calves and cutting out beef stuff, I noticed none of the boys would ride next to me on the side where the wind blew away from me. They always stayed on the opposite side. Then, too, I could always smell a dirty, decaying smell somewhere near me. This got to worrying me a lot. I thought it must be my throat or teeth so I asked Frank if I could go to Fort Benton to consult a doctor. "Sure, Bob," he answered, and I rode to Fort Benton and consulted two doctors, Dr. Carroll and Dr. Atchinson. They both laughed at me and said they could find nothing wrong with me, so I left Benton for the P Lazy N wagon. I had reached Harwood Lake when it began to rain. I took my slicker from the saddle and unrolled it. In it was an old hunk of beefsteak just full of maggots. Part of the slicker had already rotted away. I came

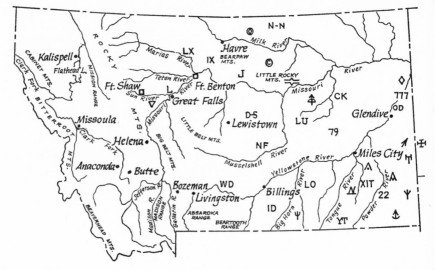

Montana ranches where Bob Kennon rode.

back to the wagon that evening but kept my counsel. I knew I was
only being paid back.

Powers and Norris bought a high-priced registered Hereford
bull for a herd bull. They bought this animal in Helena, shipping him down on a train to Big Sandy. Norris told George
Jeffries and myself to go get this bull. All went well from Big
Sandy to the P Lazy N Ranch. Here they had a big ferryboat on
the Missouri River, and we succeeded in getting him on the ferry
without any trouble. He had a ring in his nose and a strap with
which to hold him.

I was to hold him and George was to ferry the boat. We had
the bull in the middle of the ferryboat, but he jerked loose from
me and ran to the end of the boat on the same side we brought
him in on. He was so big and heavy that he lowered the end of
the boat until the water began flowing in. We always had a smaller boat tied to the ferryboat in case of an emergency. There was

also a cable on wheels where you could pull yourself across the river if the ferry was not working.

The ferry began going down at the end where the bull was, and the front end, where George was, began going high into the air. George decided to leave in a hurry and jumped into the small boat alongside the ferry, leaving me and the bull still on the ferry. I yelled and told him to come back with the boat, so he did and I jumped into it with him. The bull jumped off into the river when the water got too high in the ferry and swam back to the side from which we had brought him. The ferry floated down the river for some distance, landing close to Lohses' ranch house, and remained with one end sticking up in the air. Norris was greatly displeased when we told him our hard-luck story about losing his valuable bull and he sent us after him again. We had to go all the way around to bring him across the river bridge at Fort Benton. In the summertime when the river had gone down, they took teams of horses and pulled the ferry out and up onto the riverbank.

The Missouri River was very high in the spring of 1908, but when the water had gone down, George Jeffries and I went across on the cage with the cable to the opposite side of the river, curious to see what had come down. In some places the old river had been all of a half-mile wide at floodtime. We were searching around when we happened to see one of those big black wardrobe trunks. "Let's open it and see what's inside," said George. This we did and found that it contained men's clothing of expensive materials and style. There were suits of clothes, shirts, shoes, and a big, tall silk stovepipe hat. All these clothes were in good shape, just a little damp, and everything in it fit George perfectly. The only thing that fit me was the silk hat.

Norris had a big bunch of Indians working for him at what was known as the Murphy Line Camp. He had bought this fine ranch to be utilized as a hay ranch, for it would yield about two hundred tons of hay. There was a big irrigation ditch on this ranch, about four or five miles from Norris' home ranch. These Indians had some children at their camps, among them a ten-year-old boy who had succeeded in building a canoe for himself and could paddle it downstream in this big irrigation ditch. One day he took off all his clothes while canoeing, reverting to the savage. He left his canoe near the Norris ranch and walked into the house just as he was. Norris was astonished and angry at such conduct, and he grabbed a razor strap and whipped the kid all the way back to the irrigation ditch. The poor kid couldn't paddle the canoe upstream and walked all the way home to the camp. About thirty years after this incident I met this same boy in Helena, now of course grown to manhood. He came up to me on the street and said he knew me.

"You're Kickin' Bob who was at the P Lazy N the day I paddled my canoe down to Norris' ranch," he said.

We both laughed about this and he said, "Old Bill Norris sure did give me a tannin' with that razor strap."

On the P Lazy N Ranch there was a big barn with a bunkhouse built onto it. This was at the home ranch on the Judith River. Here also there was a big store and post office. Milsap and I were standing in the bunkhouse door when Norris drove up in his buckboard. He tied the lines to the seat and walked around in front to let the neck yoke down.

"I'll bet you he don't unhook the tugs," I said to Milsap.

"I'll call that bet," he answered. "No man would unhook a team until he unhooked the tugs."

George Jeffries had come along by this time and said he would hold the stakes. I had bet ten dollars and Milsap had called. Norris undid the hames, the bellybands, and whatever else was necessary to get the harness off the horses' backs and then threw it back over the dashboard. He took off the bridles and turned the team into the pasture near the barn, then walked to the house.

"Take your ten dollars," said Milsap. "That's the first time I ever saw anything quite like that."

When Norris wanted to hitch his team to the buckboard, he would bridle the team, back them in where they belonged, put on the harness, hook up the tongue and neck yoke and get the lines loose from the seat, jump in, and be off on his business.

CHAPTER XVI

Kid Curry

IN MONTANA there are two ranges of Rocky Mountains: the large main range of the towering, magnificent Rockies and the Little Rockies north of Lewistown. These are the miniature range of mountains, rugged scenery, jutting right out of the prairie. One can drive northeast from Lewistown and cross a ferry on the Missouri River. Most of this drive is over a dirt road, and nestled back in the hills you will find Landusky and Zortman. Today they are old gold camps, practically deserted, each having only a handful of citizens. This section is now mostly a mecca for deer hunters and tourists.

In 1894, Pike Landusky found pay dirt here and founded the town which was named for him. Landusky was as wild a town as could be found in Montana. Pike Landusky himself was tough and it was said he had whipped every man in that section of the country. He had killed two men with his bare fists and was so battle scarred himself he was hard to look at. This did not stop him, however, from marrying a widow with four grown daughters.

One of these daughters, Elfie, fell in love with Lonny Logan and became the mother of a son without the benefit of clergy, and this caused a feud between Landusky and the Logan brothers. When Lonny and Harvey were arrested for cattle theft and held for trial, they were placed in charge of Landusky, who abused them and testified against them at the trial. But in spite of all this, they were released.

On Christmas of 1894 there was a giant celebration. Johnny Logan, who owned a ranch near Landusky, donated the use of his large new barn for a dance and Lonny, a pretty good fiddler, furnished the music. There was plenty of liquor for everyone, but most of the citizens left for home after the first night. Pike Landusky, the Logans, and several others continued with the celebration and were still drunk on December 27 when all the trouble started.

A little one-legged man from Great Falls, named Jew Jake, had recently opened a combination clothing store and saloon. Harvey and Lonny Logan, with a friend named Jim Thornhill, had returned to town and were in this store and bar. When Pike Landusky entered and passed by them, Harvey struck him on the jaw, knocking him down. Lonny and Thornhill whipped out their guns to prevent interference. Both Harvey and Pike had on guns but they did not try to use them. Pike was handicapped by being much older and by a heavy overcoat he was wearing. The younger man had all the advantage, and he was beating the older man's face into a pulp.

When Pike could stand no more of it, he tried to get his gun from beneath his overcoat. When he did this, Logan shot him dead. In spite of the fact that Pike was a fighter, he had lots of friends, and when Harvey saw the look on their faces, and knowing he had started the fight, he and all the Logans and their friend Thornhill left town in a hurry.

More than sixty years ago a gang of train robbers known as the Wild Bunch was active in this section. It was led by Butch Cassidy, and with him at one robbery were Harvey Logan, Harry Longabaugh, and Camilla Hanks. The Logan boys had assumed the name of Curry, and Harvey was commonly called Kid Curry. On July 3, 1901, at 2:00 P.M., there was a holdup of the Great Northern train near a town called Wagner, 196 miles east of Great Falls.

A little more than a year before this, on February 28, 1900, Kid Curry's brother Lonny had been killed at the home of an aunt at Dodson, Missouri, while dodging Pinkerton detectives and local officers. The detectives had trailed him from Harlem, Montana, as a known participant in a train robbery on June 2, 1899, nine miles west of Rock Creek and between Le Roy and Wilcox, Wyoming. Curry and four other outlaws and his cousin Bob Lee, also known as Bob Curry, blew up the safe in the express car of the Union Pacific train and escaped with about thirty thousand dollars. This holdup didn't net them any fortune, however, for the loot proved to be unsigned currency.

The Logan brothers returned to Montana to seek revenge on Jim Winters for having them arrested in Landusky. They went to Winters' ranch on January 16, 1896, to kill him, but he had been warned and was ready for them with a shotgun filled with scrap iron. Johnny Logan was killed instantly and the others fled, but Harvey Logan returned some time later and killed Winters. Within a few miles of Landusky are the graves of Landusky, Johnny Logan, and Jim Winters.

I knew Lonny Curry well when he owned and operated a saloon in Harlem with a partner named Hart. Lonny was a fiddler at all the dances and was always kind to everyone who needed help. Before the Wyoming holdup, he had a visitor at his saloon, and after this visitor left, Curry told Hart: "I'm going away for about a month and want you to take care of the place."

Lonny didn't return until the early part of July, 1899, and he had another fellow with him whom he introduced around town as his brother, Bob Curry, but this fellow was really his cousin, Bob Lee. Lonny had a one-thousand-dollar bill which he asked the Harlem postmaster to cash. The postmaster told him he didn't have that much cash but he could send the bill down to the bank at Fort Benton and the amount would be returned the next day in smaller bills. But the money was not returned from the bank at Fort Benton because the detectives had gotten in touch with all the banks and they were on the lookout for the Wyoming holdup money.

The Harlem postmaster had been tipped off about the money too, so when Lonny came to the post office for his money, the postmaster told him it must have missed the train. That same night, the detectives came to Harlem. They persuaded the postmaster to go to the Curry saloon and show them which fellow was Curry. They went to the saloon and played a game of pool, but Lonny knew his danger. He spotted the strangers as detectives in an instant, and he went to a room where his cousin Bob Lee was sleeping and said, "We'll have to drift, Bob."

"Let's shoot it out," said Lee.

"No, we're goin'," answered Lonny.

So they slipped out the back door, got two good saddle horses, and headed south. At the Milk River bridge south of Harlem was a storekeeper who operated a general store.

"Do you want to buy my saloon?" asked Curry. "My mine's for sale for one thousand dollars, too."

"I only have about three hundred dollars," said Ringwald, the storekeeper.

"I'll take your three hundred dollars, and you sign a note for the balance made payable to Jim Thornhill," answered Curry.

Jim Thornhill was a brother-in-law of the Currys and a successful cattleman, held in high repute by everyone, though it was later proved he was mixed up in some of the escapades of the Logans. I often stopped at his ranch home. A fellow known to everyone in the community as the Gallopin' Swede, because he was such a fast walker, made his home with the Thornhills. In 1903–1904, Thornhill sold out his holdings and moved to Arizona. The Gallopin' Swede got a job as a mail carrier out of

Lewistown, carrying mail to all the smaller post offices along the way, Rocky Point being one of them.

Lonny Curry still loved Pike Landusky's stepdaughter, Elfie, and did not wish to leave without giving her some money, and so rode up into the Little Rockies where she lived. Their two children had been sent away to a convent school in the East, far away from the unlawful pursuits of the Curry gang. They wanted their children to become educated, right-living individuals.

Lonny was going under the assumed name of Frank Miller when he was trailed to Dodson, Missouri, and killed by a posse. Tom Clary, whom I knew very well and valued highly as a friend, was sheriff in old Chouteau County when that county was comprised of what is now Hill, Blaine, and Phillips counties. Sheriff Clary said he was positive the body of the slain man was that of Lonny Curry, even though his appearance was changed somewhat by his mustache having been shaved off. Clary reported on his return to Fort Benton that Bob Curry (Lee) was also under arrest at Cheyenne, Wyoming.

The *Kansas City Star* reported the killing and identification of Lonny Curry, yet many people who knew the Curry boys still maintain that Lonny took part in the Wagner holdup and was later seen alive. Some still stoutly maintain that he operated his saloon in Harlem on July 3, 1901. Even his "wife," who visited in Landusky, told the Landusky reporter of the *Phillips County News* that he couldn't have taken part in the Wagner holdup because at that time he was several hundred miles away.

Ruel Horner and Jack (Josh) Gardipee were two early-day stage drivers in the Little Rockies. They each hauled twelve hundred pounds of gold bullion a month and for payday at the mines regularly brought in from eight to ten thousand dollars in cash. They were never held up. For many years Ruel Horner tended bar at Landusky, always wearing his hat. Jack Gardipee was a cowhand working on the Shonkin Ranch for a period of several years. He now makes his home in the friendly little town of Square Butte, located in Chouteau County. Jack makes an annual pilgramage to Zortman each summer where he visits numerous relatives and recalls the old-time incidents of his life.

CHAPTER XVII

Charlie Russell

I WAS REPPING for the 79 at the Big State wagon in the Judith Basin when Charlie Russell was a night-hawk. He had held this same job for eleven years. Pete Vann, Bill Skelton, and Teddy Blue Abbott were also there. In later years Vann and Skelton became well-to-do cattlemen in the Geyser country, and Abbott ran cattle below Fort Maginnis.

We had camped on a high divide west of Judith River, about fifteen miles from the river, where there were a number of big springs. Charlie Russell was as lousy as a pet coon. Pete Vann and Bill Skelton told him to pull off all his clothes and lay them on some anthills near by.

"Will that take care of the situation?" asked Charlie.

"Yes, the ants will eat all the lice," Bill Skelton answered.

Charlie pondered over this a second or two, then began undressing, putting his clothes on the anthills. The first thing he pulled off was his hat, then his coat and shirt, then off went his pants, lastly his boots. The ants sure had a feast and devoured all the lice. Bill Skelton and Pete Vann walked down to the roundup wagon, bringing back some cottonwood sticks and boards. They drove the stakes into the ground, tied the boards to the sticks with some rawhide strings, took a piece of charcoal from the fire, and printed this sign:

LOUSE CREEK BENCH

This bench is known by that name to this day.

Shortly after I became acquainted with Charlie, he quit riding for a living. Ma Nature seemed to have it planned that he was to make his big pile with his brushes and palette.

He left his mark of friendship and the touch of his genius in many places, and of course in the saloons all over the range country. Every little cow town had his wonderful buffalo, his Indians, his bears, and the pictures of us cowpokes. Dozens of times we found these pictures which he had given to his old friends to decorate their homes and their saloons. Almost everyone knew Charlie, and he visited a lot during the active times of the year and when the weather was good. You could usually locate him every summer at some of his old stomping grounds. The roping and cutting range, the branding corral, and the chuck wagon— these were the things he painted in winter at home in his studio, but in the summer he liked to visit around and take back again these fresh memory pictures of all he loved.

I'll never forget the night I first met Charlie. It happened in Lewistown, and as well as I remember it was in 1897. It seems to me this was the year we had so many good times in Lewistown, when we would come in for a fight with those gold miners from Gilt Edge. I'll certainly always remember that this was the year I met Charlie, and the night when all the drinking went on at the bar next to the stage station, a plenty popular bar for fellows who waited for the usually late stage.

We cowboys came in from Kendall and at this time we were flush with money and with spare time to enjoy ourselves. It was late summer and just before fall roundup. We were itching to try our luck at a few games and have a few drinks before the fellows from Gilt Edge would get into town. There were some among us who would never rest until they could beat up some of these cooty miners, who were due in town this Saturday night. They had been paid off, and were anxious for some poker and whiskey.

Charlie was a great lover of animals, especially the wild ones, so we did a lot of trapping that night over the bar. Looking back to that night, he seemed no different from the rest of us, for he was jolly and full of the devil. He was dressed just like other riders except for that old red sash he always wore. He asked repeatedly how this or that range was, who had sold out their spreads, how the water and grass were, and all those things a range man's always interested in. I'm sure that, though we all liked his pictures, he hadn't the faintest idea of their worth, nor did we appreciate the genius who sat that night laughing and exchanging stories of the Judith and the Musselshell roundups with us.

It was very hot inside, so Charlie and I strolled outside. He pointed up the road and remarked that the dust being stirred up must be the stage coming in. But he was wrong, for it was a buckboard coming in at a good trot. As the vehicle pulled to a stop, we recognized the driver as a rancher who lived not very far from town. He was a good fellow, but had a reputation for getting drunk and staying on a spree for weeks at a time when he got to town. Tonight, though, he refused to be drawn inside the saloon and declared he had come in to meet a friend who was due on the stage from Great Falls.

His name was Hugh McIver and it was whispered around by the hangers-on at the bar that he was waiting for a lady whom he had never met but to whom he had been writing all winter and spring, getting her name and address from one of those "mail-order bride" papers. He was dressed up in a new brown suit, white shirt, green tie, and new hat. His boots were polished to a gloss. He seemed nervous and kept asking about the stage from Great Falls. I was told that he had driven in from his homestead near Lewistown to meet his mail-order bride, whom he had found through that magazine called *Heart and Hand*.

Charlie got quite a kick out of this story, and the homesteader took on a new importance and interest for all of us you may be sure. In spite of his extreme nervousness, we couldn't persuade him to take a drink. I think it might have been all right if it hadn't been for those miners, who now began to arrive in ore wagons, buggies, and on horseback. As soon as these roughnecks found out that Hughie was waiting for a new bride, he didn't have a chance to stay sober. They dragged him inside bodily and started filling him with whiskey. As soon as he got a little too much, he started giving all his secrets away, and soon he pulled out the lady's picture and these miners were having a regular picnic with him.

Meanwhile, where was the Great Falls to Lewistown stage?

Now perhaps I should tell you that at any season of the year it was a long, hard trip. It had been a wet spring and during the summer we had had a lot of rain in the early part, so that when we did get the hot weather, the sun baked these deep ruts and chuckholes into a mighty rough road. It took a good twenty-four hours to make the trip with a six-horse team. Of course the teams were changed at the relay stations, which were really ranches or very small cow towns. From Great Falls to Lewistown the stopping places, as I remember, were Belt, Cora Creek, Spion Kop, Old Geyser, Old Stanford, and then, I believe, some ranch halfway between Stanford and Lewistown. Anyway, when travelers got that far, they were pretty sore from the bumps of the road and strangers always asked: "My God, how much farther to Lewistown?"

On this night at the saloon in Lewistown, Charlie tried to talk Hughie into leaving the boys and taking a walk out in the air, but Hughie refused to do so. He showed Charlie and me the lady's picture, though it was now much the worse for the handling and grabbing of the miners, who were bent on pestering the bridegroom. After looking at the photo, which had been done in St. Jo in big-city style, we could see that the lady was certainly a "good looker," to quote Charlie. We both had our doubts, though, as to whether this was the girl Hughie would actually get. This had happened before and it wasn't the first time that a lady sent some beauty's picture instead of her own.

This one was dark haired, with flashing white teeth and large, dark eyes which gazed somewhat boldly at us. "A very flashy sort of gal"—that was what we all agreed. She was dressed fit to kill in white flounces and laces and ribbons, which was the fashion of city ladies at this time. Upon her curls was perched a big white hat, and she carried an umbrella—I think they called it a parasol.

On the back of the photo, Hughie told us, were the full instructions as to how she was to be met at Lewistown and they

146

stated she would be wearing this same outfit and carrying in the other hand a bird cage with her pet canary in it. We later had reason to recall this parasol and bird-cage arrangement.

Now the part about meeting her made Charlie laugh, as he could see that this girl thought she might get lost or the crowd would be so large that Hughie would have a time finding her. We decided that it was time to do something drastic before this lady arrived, for the least we could do would be to see that she was given a decent reception, no matter how things turned out afterward for Hughie. Charlie and the bartender cooked up a plan, and after everyone had a round of drinks the bar was closed and we all went outside to cool off and wait for the stage. There was less objection to this arrangement than we feared, and we hoped we could sober Hughie up out there. To tell the truth, I was for taking him over to the hotel where I had gotten a room earlier in the day and putting him to bed, but Charlie was against this and someone went out promising to get back with some black coffee. Then Charlie spied the water trough where we tended the horses and stage teams and declared that a dip in this cold spring water would be just the thing, but we had to act quick for the stage was due any time. We had Hughie between us, and he refused to even take a drink of the water, though we set a good example by drinking freely of it as it trickled down into the trough. At a sign from Charlie, we gave him a good push and he sprawled into the trough, choking and blubbering.

If we had not gotten him out when we did, he would surely have drowned. We tried to dry him off, but it was so hot this didn't take much effort. Lord, was he mad! It was getting dark by now and all of us went into the stage station and left him outside raving. Charlie said he felt a sort of kinship with anyone coming from Missouri and he was going to see that this lady was treated well.

At last a yell went up as the stage was coming in, with great clouds of dust whirling along the horizon. We rushed out and could hear the rumble of the vehicle and the rattle of the harness on the six-horse team.

Lanterns were brought out and hung up, as was the custom when the passengers were to get out. Of course there was so much pushing and so much chatter and noise that Charlie and I were left way back in the crowd. We craned our necks and pushed too, so we at least could see that a man was helping a lady down. She had on light clothes, and sure enough, Hughie was being called up front. He was there and you must know that he was beyond any sensible conversation.

Soon everyone was going into the station and here we saw that she was indeed the same gal as in the photo. I must state that a lot of fellows lost their bets, as some had bet for sure that she would not show up at all and some others that it would be a different gal. Though it was the same girl, she didn't look as fresh as her picture, for her dress was wrinkled and she seemed wilted all over. She had no hat nor parasol, and indeed no bird cage.

She saw Charlie and rushed to meet him and cuddled in his arms. She kissed him smack on the lips and knocked his Stetson off into the dust. The crowd hooted and hollered, and as Charlie tried to free himself from this unwanted situation, here came the worst-looking spectacle it has been my lot to behold. There stood Hughie, wet and very angry as he clutched the photo. He was pushed forward and introduced to the girl, but she seemed to think it was some joke and still clung to Charlie's arm. Hughie refused to claim her and demanded to see the bird cage, the hat, and the parasol. He seemed to think that he had been cheated. He was just sobering up and at that unhappy stage which makes a man really mean. It took some talking to convince both of them.

Charlie told some bystanders that she should be taken over to Ma Murphy's, who kept a respectable boarding house, and we promised her that we would see what could be done with Hughie when he became more sober. She was a swell-looking girl and no shrinking violet, but now she seemed to have a crush on Charlie and would have traded in Hughie for sure, but we told her Charlie was a married man.

The stage driver even tried to explain to Hughie that he didn't let her bring the bird cage and that it was still up in Great Falls, and that she had nearly been left behind at the halfway station near Lewistown and there she had left her hat and parasol in the rush.

Hughie finally sobered up and came to his senses, and he and his mail-order bride were married by a preacher in Ma Murphy's parlor. Often in later years Charlie would ask me how Hughie's bargain turned out. Her name was Dolly and she was known for miles around, as she bought herself a fancy top buggy and a team of matched bays which she named Granger and Rowdy. They were put up at the livery barn many times when I was there in Lewistown, and many would have paid her a top price for that fine team.

For many years Charlie's path and mine crossed often, but I didn't have the pleasure of meeting his wife until we attended the big Calgary Stampede. I could see then why he had taken up a different life from his earlier and wilder cowboy days, for she was a fine little lady. She was not only pretty, but she had wit and sparkle, often crossing us both in a good argument.

One day Charlie and I were sitting along the bank of the Missouri River where the Milwaukee Railroad depot now stands in Great Falls. As we carried on a lazy sort of general conversation, Charlie picked up a handful of adobe with his left hand and from this he fashioned a perfect image of a bear. He modeled this without even seeming to be looking at what he was doing, and when it was finished he handed it to me. I couldn't help but wonder at such genius, and I wish now I had kept it.

Another time, Charlie and I were at a cigar store, one of his favorite hangouts, next door to the Mint Saloon. Late in the afternoon his wife, Nancy, drove down in their one-horse buggy to take him home. She was sitting in the buggy, near the curb, looking at a fellow standing on the edge of the sidewalk. He had all sorts of tobacco tags on his hat. Charlie drew a picture of this character. In about a week I saw him again and he handed me this picture. It was a perfect likeness. I thanked him, and put the picture in my vest pocket, little knowing how very valuable that sketch would become as time passed. I suppose the picture just wore out there in my pocket.

Sid Willis, owner of the famous Mint Saloon in Great Falls, and Charlie were very close friends. For years the walls of the Mint were lined on either side with large Russell paintings, many of them gifts to Sid from his artist friend, many of them to pay for drinks for other friends. People from all over the United States, as well as foreign lands, paid visits to the Mint to view these paintings. Actually this place was more like an art gallery than a saloon, and here, too, were many of Charlie's finest models done in wax.

Sid was acquainted with many famous people. He and Jaycox, the Milner Livestock Company range boss, went to Texas from Arkansas on horseback. They then decided to come north with a Texas trail herd, the N Bar N outfit. Jaycox secured a job with the Milner Livestock Company, and Sid stayed on with the N Bar N, both of Glasgow, Montana. Later on he became a United States marshal, holding this job for many years. Sid passed away in the early fifties, leaving a void in the friendship of many years which cannot be easily filled. He never ceased grieving for Charlie, who had passed on many years earlier.

Charlie had come back from the Mayo Clinic and was pretty weak. He had suffered a long time from sciatic rheumatism, and now, as he said, his "old pump was givin' out." Before he died on October 24, 1926, he told his wife he wanted to be carried to the cemetery behind horses. Horse-drawn hearses had gone out of style by then and they had to search a long time before they found one in Cascade that had been stored away for years. But his wife saw that his wish was carried out.

As I stood there with the rest of Charlie's friends—which numbered into the hundreds—and watched his riderless horse and the old hearse carry his mortal remains to the cemetery, I felt a sadness that, like many another cowman's, was too deep to be put into any language. He had indeed joined the old trail riders on the "Other Side."

CHAPTER XVIII

Old Geyser

MANY YEARS AGO Pat O'Hara was an up-and-coming jovial Irishman who operated a stage station, general store, country hotel, blacksmith shop, and cattle ranch in the Judith Basin. His town was called Geyser. When I say "his town," it's a true statement, for he owned everything around there. Pat decided he needed one of those newfangled automobiles and as Great Falls was the nearest place he could buy one, he went up there to purchase it. He took his two good friends Pete Vann and Bill Skelton with him.

He bought a Ford and started out for Geyser and Home Sweet Home. A crowd in Geyser was waiting for him to get back so they could see this new horseless contraption. He seemed a long time getting back, but finally he came down the old stage road in a cloud of dust. But he didn't stop. All he did was toot the horn at his wife, Mayme, and the fellows in front of the saloon who were waiting for him. He kept right on going until he got to Greybull, Wyoming. He had to stop then, for he was out of gas. Pat explained later to his friends that he couldn't stop because "they showed me how to start it, but never told me how to stop it." Charlie drew a sketch of this trio like he did of so many other happenings.

Pat called his town Geyser because on his holdings there were a number of sulphur springs flowing warm water. Sometimes they would throw up a huge stream of water, so Pat called them geysers, thinking I suppose, of the geysers in Yellowstone Park.

Traveling men would come in on the stage, whiskey salesmen, hardware and grocery salesmen, and they would ask Pat, "How are the geysers?" Pat would always tell them, "Oh, they are due to erupt in a day or two. You'd better stay over at the hotel and see the sight."

I had been repping for a long time and came in with a lot of the boys for a night's fun at Pat O'Hara's saloon in Geyser when Indian Charlie shot up the town. Now when I speak of Old Geyser, I mean the original site of this town on the old stage road, before it was moved to the railroad.

In 1907–1908 when the Great Northern Railroad came through the Judith Basin country, Pat's old town of Geyser was left way off the line of the railroad's survey, so Pat just decided he would establish a new town on the railroad. This he did without delay. Most of the buildings from his old location, all that could be moved, were taken over to the new location. Charlie Russell drew a picture of this moving. In the picture was a wheelbarrow, and on this were a pool table, bottles of Blue Ribbon whiskey and a bottle of muscatel, poker chips and a poker table, and to top it off, he had the honorable Pat pushing the wheelbarrow.

But I am now telling about Old Geyser. Pat was the best-hearted fellow in the world. He and his wife, Mayme, ran the hotel, the saloon, and practically everything else in the burg. Pat was mayor, and sometimes there was no sheriff around, so he had to act as marshal too. The stage would bring in strangers sometimes, and he would go to his box behind the bar and get out his phony law badge, put on his coat and hat, and stroll out, smoking a cigar. This was for the protection of this little town. The stage came down from Great Falls through Belt, Armington, changed horses at old Bill Cresap's place on Cora Creek, then on to Spion Kop, then into Geyser. This was a mighty long trip at the time.

Pat's brother-in-law, Dave Rankin, was an old stage driver and chuck-wagon cook. He was also a fine fiddler and this is what he was doing in Geyser the night this Indian Charlie shot up the place. We sure got a scare, as lead was flying around like a duststorm when this half-breed Indian went on his rampage. The boys were celebrating, as we had just finished the spring calf roundup and it was well into summer. We were laying off until time to go on the beef roundup if we could make our pile last that long. The poker games were running full blast and Pat was plenty busy at the bar, even with a couple of bartenders helping him.

Indian Charlie had a way of riding his horse right into a saloon and had done this in Pat's place often. Pat soon outsmarted him, though, by putting in a door so narrow a horse couldn't get through it. I've seen fat men grunt and rip their clothes trying to get in.

We were all betting on what Charlie was going to do this night, as he was just pouring down the drinks. It seemed he could hold a barrel of whiskey. Pat had a way of watering down the Indian's drinks after he thought he was so full of fire-water he wouldn't be able to smell or taste the difference. Pat got careless, though, and on this night Charlie caught him at this trick and opened fire right there at the bar.

There was such a noise going on over at the dance hall that they didn't hear the first shots. Those at the dance were the cowboys from near-by ranches, the respectable ranchers with their wives and pretty daughters. They were hoeing it down in great style. Billy Braun had arrived a short while before the dance started with his roller organ, and though somewhat delayed by the high water of Braun Creek from a cloudburst, he was now making up for lost time. This roller organ gave the fiddlers and mouth-organ player a rest, and it made dandy music.

Luckily, Dave Rankin was just coming out after Billy relieved

154

him and was planning on wetting his parched throat over at Pat's bar. He met a scene of confusion, with everyone hollering, running, and yanking horses from the hitching rails. Knowing that Indian Charlie was in town, Dave bolted back into the dance hall and gave the word. The door of the hall was locked and the windows closed. Everyone got down low on the floor. Past experiences were recalled.

A bunch of us escaping from the bar were hunting a hiding place, but in the moonlight it was tough to find cover. Mrs. O'Hara's clean, white wash still hung on the clothesline. That morning, as we rode in, Mayme O'Hara's pretty hired girl was just hanging it out. Now we stood there a minute and here came Charlie galloping after Pat, who, of course, was making for his hotel. Somehow Pat, the washing, and Indian Charlie on his horse all got tangled up. The Indian had quit shooting by now, as he had emptied his gun. He just kept going, but when we picked Pat up there by the steps, he was sure a sight, with a pair of women's white, lace-trimmed drawers around his neck. He was fighting his head like a blindfolded bronc.

That didn't stop the dance, though, and it lasted until long past dawn. It was one of the best times I can ever remember having in Geyser. It could rain here, too, and the town got its name from a mud geyser near by. When it rained for a week, it looked like the whole town was one mud geyser.

There was one such rainy night that I'll long remember. We were getting ready for the spring roundup, and a bunch of us cowpunchers rode into Geyser to see that the chuck-wagon supplies were bought and loaded. Pat O'Hara told us not to be in a hurry, as the weather certainly looked threatening and a big spring rain might break at any time. He opened up the best stock he had and sure enough, we decided to have the supplies loaded by the time the rain cleared up. Anyway, we could put up the wagon sheet, which consisted of big canvas tarps over the bows which were left on the wagon at all times. We could pull out even in pouring rain and get the stuff safely back to the home ranch.

We piled up the slabs of bacon, paper bags of navy beans, as well as those big lima beans, rice, oatmeal, corn meal, sacks of flour, coffee, syrup, soda, and baking powder, which was then put up in paper boxes instead of tin cans like it is today. There were dried prunes, dried apples, sugar, and all kinds of staple foods and items necessary to a cook and his chuck wagon. Pat wrote it all down and hung the bill up on the back wall—he never worried about the pay, as ranchers had big accounts and paid after shipping time in the fall.

The half-breed helper put it all at the end of the storehouse and said for us to go in and get it any time we were ready to leave. Pat then headed for the saloon and treated us all to the best he had. Far into the night there was plenty of fun and the fellows got drunker by the hour. Lord, how it rained! Now along toward daylight someone said it had quit raining and we had better hit for the home ranch with that load of grub. So out we went to see to the horses and the loading of this grub. One of the fellows came in and said to me, "Never mind, Bob, she's all loaded, and we're gathering the teams to hitch to the wagons."

When I heard this, I decided to see if the boys had overlooked anything. Well, that wagon was a sight, for some of those drunks had loaded every bit of that grub order, but had failed to put up the canvas tarps on the bows. The rain had ruined everything. The beans had soaked and swollen; so had the prunes and dried apples, and believe me, if you've ever cooked any, you know how they swell when soaked. They were bulging out through the box sides and mingling with the broken, soggy bean sacks. The soda and baking-powder boxes had broken open and fizzed up, the rice, flour, and oatmeal bags were soggy and turning to a doughy mass, and somebody had opened the syrup, to sample it no doubt, and left the stopper out of the jug. This mess flowed over the burlap bags of Arbuckle coffee beans, and every thing was rendered useless.

Pat heard the news and came running. "Holy Mother of God and the Saints, how did all this happen?" he yelled. But no one seemed to know. All we could do was clean it up, and here we found the canvas tarps at the bottom of the load. We dumped it all out and stocked up again from Pat's supplies.

There was a barber in Geyser who used to be very neat and particular. He took great pride in his shop and kept it up to the minute. He changed his coat every day and would clean and polish his mirrors and plate-glass window every time he had a moment of liberty from shaving and hair cutting. He hated to take care of sheepherders and had a bathhouse at the rear of his shop where he made them undress on newspapers to catch the "vermin," as he called lice. He would throw away their clothes and make them put on clean store clothes, which they had to buy before coming into his bathhouse. This was an unwritten law and the word spread among the sheepherders that one couldn't come in his front door like others if he didn't act according to these rules.

We were laughing about this barber as we rode out of town one day. There he was as he bowed and waved us good-by, outside wiping the dust off his shining barber pole. As we rode out a ways we came across a dead mule by the roadside. The boys were seized with an impulse. I thought it a good idea, too. We roped the carcass of the poor old mule and dragged it down into a coulee. When it got dark enough, we rode back to Geyser. In the meantime, we took some heavy store wrapping paper off a package one of the boys was carrying in his bag and made a sign with a heavy black pencil. We were laughing so hard we could hardly get the job done. At last it was dark enough to ride back into town dragging the mule's carcass. We put it right in front of the big window and across the door of the barbershop. The sign we stuck on the door itself for all to read was:

HERE'S WHERE I GOT MY LAST SHAVE

Folks said there was an awful lot of excitement next morning as the barber arrived at his shop at the same time his first customer for the day did. This customer happened to be a judge from Great Falls who was obliged to remain at the hotel several days on business. He was in the habit of getting his morning shave early. Imagine the barber's shame and wrath, for he prided himself on the perfect condition of his shop!

The judge helped him haul the mule off to where a hide buyer took it over. This hide dealer later told us that the barber was looking for a certain bunch of cowpunchers and it's a good thing we rode north into the Highwoods for a long stay.

CHAPTER XIX

Some Friends of Charlie Russell

I DID A LOT of riding down near Old Stanford, Old Geyser, Lewistown, and Gilt Edge. The town of Gilt Edge was smaller than many places, but it had the best sort of people and many good cowmen. It was about twelve miles from Lewistown and was not only a good cow town, but a center for a mining district.

I was visiting this part of the country in March of 1948. The people were sad when they told me that the post office was being discontinued at the end of the month. This was the distributing point for Fort Maginnis, Maiden, Musselshell, and a lot of places that are not so important as to be of historical value. For years now these little ghost towns have been dying out, or have been burnt out. Some camper, some bum, or maybe kids with careless smoking, start the fires that make an end of it. Only we who once rode this range remember them as towns of some importance.

Thinking of Gilt Edge always reminds me of Kendall, the little near-by mining town. I remember one incident when we were with the Shonkin roundup wagon. In those unfenced and thinly populated days, cattle outfits grazed all the way over the Shonkin country. If one speaks of the Shonkin country today, it means an entirely different thing: only a small area of the High-wood Mountains. But it was a big grazing range in those grand old cattle days.

Three wagons, besides ours, were camped on Salt Creek. They

were the PN Bar, the E Bar, and the 72 Bar outfits. It had been raining heavily so we rode into town to kill time and have some fun while the weather cleared up. The whole bunch of us numbered about seventy-five men. We rode in and headed for the saloons. Now this was a strange little mining town, with its alleys and streets looking just alike. There were no fences around the houses, either, and the women hung their washings out from one house to another across the alleys.

After spending three or four days in town, we were riding back to camp on the Judith River and were feeling pretty good. The weather had cleared up so the foreman came and made the rounds of the saloons, dance halls, and sporting houses, telling us to get back to the roundup wagon.

I had a big bay horse named Walt, and believe me, he was a fast and high-spirited one. As soon as I was mounted, he started out of town with me, bucking to beat hell. A miner's wife had just put out her clothes to dry on the clothesline across one of these alleys. Walt saw these fluttering clothes and he hit that line at the horn of the saddle. Since I couldn't reach in my pocket to get my knife to cut the line, we just took those clothes with us. We dragged that wash about three miles before we could get rid of it. The next time I went to Kendall, I found out that the woman was a friend's wife. They wouldn't hear of me paying for the clothes, for most of them were the baby's diapers, so I staked the kid to a twenty-dollar gold piece.

Stanford was a good little town, too, and there were a lot of good folks living near it on some fine cattle and horse spreads. There's a lot of arguments concerning the real naming of this town. The first settlers came here in the early eighties and the town was called Dubuque. That was when the first stage station was located here. It was the renaming of Stanford that got people to arguing. There was a stockman in this part of the country named J. E. Bower. He had come from a place in New York named Stanford and was supposed to have named it after his old home town. Some folks say, though, that it was named for Major J. T. Stanford of Great Falls, but the first story is considered more likely to be the truth.

Two ranchers in this section were Pete Vann and Bill Skelton, whom I have mentioned before. They were grand people and their descendants are still around on ranches in this area. Both Vann and Skelton are mentioned many times in Charlie Russell's stories. I think old Bill Skelton was what might be called a typical Westerner. He had a way of making folks feel that they were really welcome, and he was a figure in the days of the cattlemen in this area.

Bill told me once that he took up his land in 1876 or 1877. He turned the first furrow in what is now the Judith Basin Valley. Right here I'll tell you about Russell's painting *The First Furrow*. This is one of the finest of all his paintings. Russell was a great friend of the Skeltons and one time he decided to paint a picture of this subject. He took Bill Skelton for a model. It's Bill with a team of horses hitched to an old-style walking plow you see in the picture. His hair, face, and general pose are Bill to a T. His furrow is just turned, and an Indian is riding up. You can just feel the atmosphere all charged up, too, and Bill is holding his rifle to stand his ground. There are the wonderful sky and purple mountains and buttes behind them. The waiting horses begin to graze, and the grass is so real you can feel the touch of it to your boot.

Mr. Skelton was born in England. He claimed to be ten years old at the time the Civil War was declared in this country. He came to Fort Benton by boat from Sioux City. He had done some ranching in the Prickly Pear Valley, and some on the Teton, and was an ambitious man. He was kindhearted and so was his wife. She was born of pioneer stock in a covered-wagon train somewhere passing through Minnesota. Her maiden name was Vann. She, too, had come up the river to Fort Benton, but had lived near Carroll on the Musselshell River. When I knew Bill Skelton, he had some hundred head of horses and several thousand head of cattle. He passed away only a few years ago.

Pete Vann was part Indian and quite a character. He was wrangling for Horace Brewster, but he didn't like wrangling and wanted to be a rider. He hung around the herd all day riding and roping instead of catching up on his sleep, for he was a night-hawk. Wagon master Brewster got mad at Pete and told the big boss he'd like another wrangler, but wranglers were scarce and they couldn't find anyone except Charlie Russell. He had had no experience, but they put him on and he wrangled for this outfit as long as he was a cowboy.

I repped and rode for a lot of cow outfits in the Judith Basin, from Surprise Creek, Arrow Creek, Wolf Creek, Coyote Creek, and Sage Creek toward Moccasin and Utica on the Judith River. Many know that Charlie Russell's first Montana home was near Utica. This town figured quite a lot in the early times in Montana. Some folks from Utica, New York, settled here and named the town. The famous trapper and prospector Jake Hoover, who befriended Kid Russell, came up here in 1871 or 1872. He told us once in Lewistown at a stag party for Charlie Russell that he came up by boat to Benton the year after Lincoln was shot, which would be the year after the Civil War.

We did a lot of riding around these parts and I remember one time we rode to the Pig Eye Basin Ranch. Russell had a lot of old friends in and around here, though of course a lot had gone away or passed on. However, on this trip he led us up to an old cow camp to get a big roll of deer hides that an old fellow had tanned for him, but I think he was really making the trip for old memories. This old man had learned from the Indians the much-prized way of tanning those beautiful hides. Indians, even today, don't let anyone near the camp of the Blackfoot Reservation during the time of year they process these hides.

We got the hides on the way up and Charlie was as pleased as a kid with them, but the old man wouldn't take a cent for them. But if I know Charlie, he repaid him in some other way a thousand times over. While he was in the Pig Eye Basin camp he got out his painting outfit and painted on these hides instead of a canvas. Everyone in the party got one done of anything he liked. He did the head of an Indian chief for me. It was grand and I had it on the wall of my living room for years until one time my wife and I were away on a trip and some housebreaker broke in and stole it. Of course with Charlie's signature he must have sold it for a fancy price. I still have an art dealer in New York keeping a lookout to see if it will show up there when Russell collectors have those exhibitions at the big galleries. Perhaps it will never show up again, but I'd sure like to have it back.

We didn't want to tackle that road into this old camp, but Charlie could have gone in there blindfolded. There was scenery for you, and it was the toughest place to find and get into if you were not familiar with the canyon. It was on the main, or south, fork of the Judith River. Only good saddle horses and pack outfits could go in there. There were big, high, towering cliffs, just like skyscrapers of the city, and we had to ride Indian file, as the trail was so narrow. This trail was full of boulders, causing many twists and turns.

Hoover's old camp was really his claim. Like many of the pioneers, Jake had nothing but an ax to work the logs. The cabin showed that no saw was used. He had to rough it. This earthly paradise was put on those canvases by Charlie in later years as he lived them. Here is where he saw the animal fights, wild and fierce, and the tame and timid, too. He loved them all, and memory served him well.

Jake Hoover was considered one of the best hunters in Montana, and Charlie said, "He knowed more of Nature's secrets than any man I ever met." It was while Charlie was living with Hoover that he studied the native wild animals which he later depicted so well on canvas and with clay.

Though Charlie knew that Hoover was making his living hunting these animals for their skins and meat, he also knew that Hoover was not wasteful and killed only enough to live on. But Charlie rarely went hunting with him, for he was too tender-hearted to take the life of the animals he had learned to love. He liked to study them in their natural surroundings. He was content to make himself useful around the cabin, or upon the pack trips when Jake went to sell the meat and hides. Hoover was known throughout Montana as a prospector, too, and had located many gold mines, but he knew nothing about business and let others beat him out of them. He also located several valuable emerald mines.

Old Jake was in Seattle when we made this trip, but we didn't know this until we got to the old man's place where we got the deer hides. He had come back from the Klondike, where he had had some bad luck with his prospecting. He died there in Seattle in 1924 at the age of seventy-six while planning to return to Montana. The influence he had rendered as Charlie's first real friend in Montana was priceless and profound.

CHAPTER XX

Joe Sullivan, Saddle Maker

JOE SULLIVAN'S SADDLE SHOP in Fort Benton was a hanging-out place for the cowmen of that section. He was famous for his artistic saddle work. This was one of the places Charlie Russell liked to loaf, for it had everything in it that reminded him of his range days, old friends to chat with, and saddles to compare and discuss with Joe. We would sit around and relive every big event of our experiences as cowpunchers and mourn over the fact that the years had swallowed up the life we loved. As Joe buried himself with his carving and polishing, we would breathe in the smell of saddle leather, and it was sweeter to us than any perfume on earth.

This building of Joe's was old when he and his partner, Goss, moved into it. It must have been built in the sixties. It had served as a saloon–dance hall and butcher shop. These partners had come over from Deer Lodge Valley by ox team to Fort Benton sometime back in the early eighties. About three or four years later, Joe bought out his partner and from then on it was Joe Sullivan's Saddlery. He could have built up a big store, but he wouldn't leave the old place for he loved every inch of it. He made all the saddles by hand and never rushed a job, so felt no need of a new business, or to do a lot of quick work.

Joe had no equal. His first job back in Deer Lodge Valley had been to make a lot of saddles for old Con Kohrs, who had a big spread and needed a lot of good saddles. Saddles had to be built mighty tough in the old range days, but cowmen liked them beautiful, too, so Joe became a master in combining these two features. He could put on carved roses that took a horseman's eye. He had set up his business on less than four hundred dollars, he told me once. Often he hired ten or twelve men to help him. The Royal Northwest Mounted Police once gave him an order for five hundred saddles. He made them according to their special requirements and they were highly pleased. Joe had their letter of praise and thanks tacked up on his dusty wall for years. He was very proud of this, as the Mounted Police were most particular about their equipment.

He had a knack of pleasing every type of rider and could read character by what a man said about his riding and his work. Charlie used to say that Joe had an eye like a camera, and he never forgot a face. Once in a while the artist in Charlie would suggest some change in the design of a saddle and he and Joe would work night and day on it.

I guess there are a lot of folks these days who think making a saddle is an easy job, but this is not so, even to an expert. There are a lot of parts to a saddle, and Joe did all his work by hand. There is the tree, the swell, the seat, the horn, skirt, rig, stirrups, and cinch, not to mention the carving of the leather and the embossed work. Some were two-toned and many of the fellows like these. Some also wanted a special saddle made with a Mexican roping horn.

I wish I could picture that place of Joe's, hung with straps of leather and the benches and tables piled high with it. It was a hanging-out place for the cowhands, especially the more settled ones. They squatted on the floor, some closer than others to the spittoon, for Joe was strict about tobacco juice on his floor. It was a sad day indeed for Joe when leather got high in price and scarce in quantity, for he never used anything but the best of materials.

He made me my last beautiful saddle in the twenties, and I still have it at the ranch.

Here in Fort Benton Charlie found the inspiration for his paintings of the old fort. We would talk and figure out angles on the life and times of the fur trader. Charlie saw in his heart the old fort, and he certainly made a swell job of it. Such color and space and reality he put upon his canvas, just as though it stood there for him to copy. But remember, it was his gift to see these things as they were in the days of his red brother.

Two of his paintings which I believe sold for a great price were the ones which he called *Salute to the Robe Trade,* and *The Wagon Boss.* The first-mentioned was purchased by the Mounted Police of Montana, but *The Wagon Boss* is my favorite of the two, for it shows old Chinaman Hill so plainly and the old fort below on the river. The natural richness of color and the true-to-life action of horses and riders, both Indian and white, are priceless. Charlie's storehouse of memories allowed him to draw upon it as long as he lived—for it was real to him. He had lived it.

Often he would sit and sketch while we talked. He carried a bunch of small cards in his pockets and when he had an idea, he would sketch it. Often it was something he would think of in Joe's shop. I wish I had these sketches now, for they would be priceless.

Once someone stole a saddle from Charlie while he was visiting here in Benton. Some bachelors he knew had a small house there, and though it had no barn, it did have a fenced yard. Charlie never bothered with a livery stable and was in the habit of throwing off his saddle onto the back porch and turning his horse into the yard. One night someone made off with the saddle, and though it was one he had bought in Helena, it was a valuable one. The sheriff was all for riding out after the thief, as he was anxious to please Charlie and to test the new deputies he had just sworn in. But Charlie wouldn't hear of it.

"Let 'em have it. They must have been in one hell of a spot for needin' a saddle," he said.

Someone said it was an Indian who had been stealing whiskey from a warehouse there in Benton, but Charlie only laughed and said, "No Injun would stop for a saddle. He'd just jump on the nearest cayuse bareback, without even a bridle, and be gone in a flash."

There was no habit of the Indian that Charlie did not understand and sympathize with.

As long as I knew Joe Sullivan, he never worried about locking up things for fear of thieves. When he was ready, he would put on his Stetson, shut the door, and call it a day. The sheriff warned him again and again about the valuable saddles which often remained in the shop for some time before their new owners would call for them. There was a lot of equipment and supplies, too, which were worth a lot of money, but the only theft ever committed here that I know of was a knife stolen from a window sill. It was one of those very sharp knives which Joe used on the leather, and a half-breed, seeing it there one day, decided it was just what he needed. It was later recovered by the sheriff in Havre. An Indian had carved up another one pretty badly in a fight, and after the trial, it was learned, through this breed's confession, that the knife was the one he had stolen from the saddlery here in Benton. One morning the lawman arrived at the shop and told Joe that he was returning the knife, but Joe would have none of it and told him to toss if off the bridge into the Missouri.

Speaking of Sullivan making those good saddles for the Northwest Mounted Police, this, along with other trade between Montana and Canada, had meant a friendship of many years. Today this is still so, the feeling growing stronger as the years have passed. From old Fort Benton on the southern end, north to Fort Whoop-Up, near where the town of Lethbridge now stands, this old trail was the first common link between Montana Territory and the province of Alberta. It was a trail of bull teams and bullwhackers, and over it the courageous old pioneer Jack Lee carried mail with a buggy and single horse. In this way the people of these two countries came to know, to trust, and to help one another. Today the people of Great Falls and all the Canadian cities to the north of us are one big friendly family.

In the fall of 1874, Colonel James MacLeod, with a company of Mounted Police, made the one-thousand-mile trip from eastern Canada to bring law and order to this wild and untamed country. Fort MacLeod was the westernmost fort of the Mounties. Winter came early in 1874 and this company of Mounties had a very short supply of provisions. They couldn't return to eastern Canada for more supplies, and the only place they could hope to receive help was Fort Benton. Colonel MacLeod and his party arrived at the Montana fort and acquired all the necessary help in obtaining all the supplies they needed for that long, hard winter on the Canadian prairie. This was the first link of friendship formed between us and our Canadian neighbors.

In early times there was quite a thriving trade carried on smuggling Chinamen into the United States from Canada, mostly to Fort Benton. The settlers along the Teton River were, for the most part, French Canadians. They were very industrious people, establishing good homes, raising cattle and horses for their income.

One Frenchman's name was Clemo and he was driving into Fort Benton to sell his eggs. It was a hot summer and there had been a terrible rainstorm, with fierce lightning and heavy hail falling. Old Clemo had been forced to abandon his team and wagon and take cover under a leaning rock cliff. The fierce wind drove the hailstones right into the rocks near him and lightning lit up the entire picture, though it was black as night from the heaviness of the storm. Then it subsided quickly, as storms do in this part of the country, and the sun came out, quite hot again as he made his way along the rain-washed road toward Fort Benton. Just as he was coming down the big hill, he looked into the coulee below and saw what looked like a pile of hides or buffalo robes.

Clemo pulled up the team and went over the side of the bank to look, and there under this pile of buffalo robes were huddled two Chinamen, their braided hair sticking out like pigtails. It scared him half to death, but he said nothing to these fellows, who were also very frightened from all their experiences in the storm. They must have been knocked senseless from the toss over the bank and had just huddled there. Beyond this was the driver of the team. Both man and beasts had been struck by lightning and killed. The spring wagon was a complete wreck. Clemo hurried in to Benton and brought out the law officers, who took the Chinamen into custody, later returning them to Canada. To this day this hill is known as Chinaman Hill.

CHAPTER XXI

Tragedies

THERE WAS a lot of fine cattle range around Martinsdale and White Sulphur Springs, though about the time I left the sheep men had begun to come in. It was the most Godforsaken place in winter because of the terribly deep snow, but the cowboys liked it. The snow would get so deep a fellow couldn't get out to go to town, and we played it smart and usually stayed in some town all winter until more work opened up on the roundups or horse wrangling started in early spring. Old Martinsdale was a good place, as it had plenty of saloons, and being right in the center of a wonderfully prosperous stock-raising district, there were plenty of cowmen hanging around. Located at the confluence of the three forks of the Musselshell River, it was about forty miles from the county seat and about sixty miles from Big Timber.

There was a stage line running from Martinsdale to White Sulphur Springs, but it often had to be abandoned for weeks at a time in winter. It was beautiful here in summer, and it was the grandest hay country in the state. Stock never suffered for the lack of feed.

Martinsdale and White Sulphur Springs were both good towns, and had a lot more than the Basin towns as far as accommodations and amusements. They had good stores, harness and wagon makers, blacksmith shops, a doctor's office, and a livery stable. White Sulphur Springs was trying to be recognized as a great health and pleasure resort. It began to realize its dream when a man from Germany arrived in 1949 and dickered to get hold of these springs for just such a place. He said the waters were even better than a famous resort in Germany.

If a man loves mountain country—and what he-man don't—this is the spot. Clear creeks and rivers full of fish, even though the good highway brings so many people that they must eventually be depleted. Good hunting, too, is in this part of the Rocky Mountains. Indians call it the "Good Medicine Country." Often we would come through and stop to parley with the camps of Indians. They were the Assiniboins and the Yanktons. The old chiefs claimed that this was powerful medicine, as they brought their people in here to drink of the healing springs, and then they would rest and live easily off the plentiful game while they were cured of their illnesses.

The town itself was about seventy-four miles east of Helena and about fifteen or twenty miles southeast of old Jim Brewer's pre-emption claim. Here was an old trading post called Gaddes Trading House. Fort Logan was first called Brewer's Springs, though now it is White Sulphur Springs. The town is listed as being founded in 1881.

I recall that it was during a big chinook in March after a terribly cold and blizzardly winter that we found the bodies of a young mother and her little girl. A bunch of us had been staying in the town of Martinsdale at the old Heggins Hotel most of the winter and we were plumb crazy to get out so we went down to the livery stable to get our horses and take a ride out of town. We had been cooped up so long that we were starting to fight and snap at each other, what we called "cabin fever." The barn man was not pushing us for his bills, but we sure were going to have a big one in the spring when we did get a job. That is how they were in those times: they would trust a man on his word. They never lost much on a cowboy, as they considered a barn bill almost a sacred responsibility in caring for a pet saddle horse. We always paid up as soon as we got our pay.

We started out in high spirits, for it was wonderful to be out on a horse again. They were mighty frisky, too, and kept prancing and shying at things. My friend George Ellis was with me and we were in the lead, just a short way out near some prospectors' shacks and cabins, when we found those frozen bodies.

The snow was melting and high water running in streams everywhere. My horse started shying and I had to rein him sharply. I saw this woman's blue dress first, and there they were, uncovered and exposed. It sure was a sad sight. We pulled up the horses and got off to examine the bodies closer. The woman was young. I don't think she could have been thirty years of age, and the little girl looked to be about eight.

The rest of the boys came thundering up, yelling like mad, but when they saw the look on our faces and what was on the ground, it sobered them up. They were struck dumb. A couple of the boys said they remembered seeing the little girl, too. They remembered the mother wearing the nice beaver coat.

The bodies were not in too bad condition, and while some of us went ahead to tell the sheriff, the other boys brought saddle blankets to wrap around the bodies. They carried these as best they could, but they had a bad time with the horses and in the end had to carry the bodies in on a homemade stretcher.

The townspeople were generous and helped us bury the two when we took up a collection. No one knew anything about the woman and her child, except that she was looking for her husband, who was supposed to be mining over at Barker. He must have deserted them, and was perhaps no good. We believed she was asking the help of the old prospectors down near those cabins and hoped to get over to Barker when she was caught in this blizzard. These things still happen today, and a blizzard will blind and freeze one a few rods from a fellow's home.

The sheriff kept the gold wedding ring in his safe for a long time, but no one could ever find a trace of the identity of these two unfortunates. The bodies lie in the old burial ground awaiting Judgment Day.

There were some terrible killings over there at Barker, too. Gold always causes them, and in those days things were pretty secret. You couldn't get away with some of it today, but Barker was a booming and wide-open town at that time.

Late one afternoon we were riding in the Smith River country looking for a horse spread and stallion ranch which we had heard about. We planned to look their horses over and perhaps add to our string. Every one of us loved horses and looked forward to a pleasant trip over there. It was terribly hot that day and we were just scorching, except when we would get off and lounge in the shade or drink at a spring along the road. We took a short cut across country and this is how we had so much trouble finding this spread.

Finally we spotted it across the valley. It looked like a good-sized spread—whitewashed buildings and lots of corral space and barns. Horses were grazing near by, a good-sized band of them. We made short work of the miles, for hunger was spurring us on. A few head of milk stock were bawling near the shed and calves answering them. It was milking time. I got off and opened the gate and we (there were about five of us) rode into the yard.

Except for a barking dog, the place looked very lonesome. The dog seemed to be trying to tell us something, for he would run up to us, whining and wagging his tail, then he would run up to the kitchen door and again back to us.

There was a nice kid about fifteen years old riding with us, and taking the dog in hand, he said he would go up to the house. We were all heading for the springhouse for a drink of water. He called back once to us that something stunk awful bad, but we yelled back that perhaps it was a dead coyote or wolf. There were also some pelts hanging on a fence that looked pretty nasty. The kid was on the porch when he yelled to us, and the next time we looked, he came staggering out of the open door of the kitchen, moaning something. I took care of him as he fainted dead away. The others discovered the body of a man, which had been lying there for days it seemed. He had shot himself. I tried to identify the body, but it was no one I could remember and the body was almost past recognition anyway. I held my breath as we looked around to make sure no one else was there. He must have been a hired hand looking after things while the owners were away. Each of us had sure lost our appetites. We had to ride all the way back to White Sulphur Springs to notify the authorities, and we never did learn who he was.

CHAPTER XXII

Old Fort Benton

So MANY of my stories center around Fort Benton and the Missouri River country that I feel I should tell you something of its background. Fort Benton was, and still is, the county seat of Chouteau County. This county was named for Pierre Chouteau, Jr., whose son Charles Pierre came up the Missouri in 1859. There's a town over on the Teton, too, named for him. Charles Pierre Chouteau was aboard the first steamboat to come up the Missouri as far as old Fort McKenzie (Fort Brûlé), which was located about twelve miles below Benton. He came on up to Fort Benton from there by land. He said in a report to the Secretary of War that he was sure the trip from St. Louis to Fort Benton could be made in less than thirty-five days, though his own trip had taken much longer than that.

One cannot speak of the American fur trade of the Far West without mentioning the Chouteau family. The first famous Chouteaus were, of course, Auguste and Jean Pierre. They were fur traders, and Auguste Chouteau was a founder of St. Louis, Missouri. A. P. Chouteau had trading posts in what is now Oklahoma, and Pierre Chouteau and his son Charles Pierre engaged in the fur trade on the Missouri River and some of its tributaries. Many places in different states bear the name of Chouteau. A famous landmark in Fort Benton today is an old hotel called the Chouteau House.

This old river town of Fort Benton was once the hub of Montana's commerce. During fur-trade days, the gold rush, the livestock boom, it was known all over the West. Someone once said that in the early days "all trails led to Fort Benton." This is not exactly correct, but the reverse was more nearly so: "All trails led out of Fort Benton."

Stock raising was in its infancy in Montana in 1872. A few years before, W. S. Stock located a ranch on the Teton four miles west of town to raise cattle and horses. John Lepley, Henry Austin, Patrick Murphy, and George Moore were among those starting dairy and stock farms.

Thirty-three boats brought freight for Fort Benton, but only twenty-five made the full trip; the remainder discharged freight at Cow Island. Boats arrived from Bismarck, Yankton, St. Louis, and Pittsburgh. The 1,200-ton *Kate Kinney,* biggest steamboat to dock at Fort Benton, came in from Yankton with 250 tons of freight on May 29. The *Fanny Tatum* set a cargo-carrying record (up to 1877) when she unloaded 404 tons of freight on July 9. The *Fanny Tatum* set some sort of record, too, in length of trip, leaving St. Louis April 7, running time fifty-six and a half days, although she had hit the Omaha bridge and broken a shaft.

Captain Bill Massie brought in the *Benton* from Bismarck on May 31 in eleven days and one hour for a speed record on that run. That record stood until I. G. Baker's crack new packet *Red Cloud* took her shakedown trip to Benton on June 22, turned about for Bismarck, and blew for her second landing on July 11 with a nine-day trip out of Bismarck, Captain Massie handling her. On July 28 the *Red Cloud* was back for another speed record of eight days and seventeen hours. Massie was sitting in a poker game with Wild Bill Hickok in Deadwood when Hickok was killed, and the bullet which went through his head went into Massie's forearm.

Fares from Bismarck were twenty-five dollars for deck passengers and thirty-five dollars for cabin passage. The *Peninah* became the first and perhaps the only steamboat to navigate the

Marias River. Drawing only nineteen inches, she had an easy five-mile trip up the river to get 325 bales of buffalo robes for T. C. Power.

Upbound freight totaled 4,648 tons valued at $1,394,400, plus 1,025 tons for the Canadian government worth $310,000. The Mounted Police were supplied by the I. G. Baker Company for years. Down freight was 1,530 tons, including 1,225 tons of ore. The steamboats brought thousands of passengers and tons of freight to Montana and in turn took lighter but richer cargoes of furs; robes; gold dust, bullion, and high-grade ores; cattle and grains; the few hundred successful miners who wished to leave the lonely country; *voyageurs,* whose task was done; and the misfits and weaklings who turned back from the task of building new states out of the wilderness.

Like the spokes of a wheel, trails radiated from Fort Benton, head of steamboat navigation, all over Montana. A few crumbling adobe walls of an old trading post; a riprapped riverbank where the boats used to dock; a few deep-rutted and grass-grown trails of the old-time freighters which the plow has not touched; a few relics, pictures, and keepsakes—these are what Fort Benton has to show to make good its boast of being "The Birthplace of Montana." These few physical mementos of the old days, the memories of the old-timers, and the growing consciousness of our people of the stories of the past bring a touch of pride to Fort Benton citizens today.

The *Nellie Peck* was the first steamboat to arrive at Fort Benton in 1872, on May 18, and the *Sioux City* closed the season on August 7, but the river trade gradually declined within a few years.

If a fellow looks at a picture of these old boats and gives it a good study, he can tell that their builders used some good judgment in making them for this river work. I shiver, though, when I think how frail they really were and what terrible firetraps

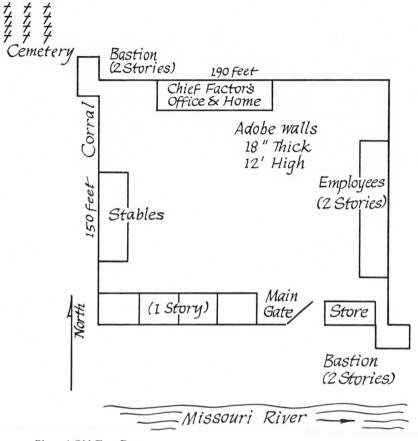

Cemetery

Bastion (2 Stories)

190 feet

Chief Factor's Office & Home

Adobe walls
18" Thick
12' High

Corral

150 feet

Stables

Employees (2 Stories)

North

(1 Story)

Main Gate

Store

Bastion (2 Stories)

Missouri River

Plan of Old Fort Benton.

they could be. They were well enough built and some were real fancy according to the photos on record today. They had a broad bottom and a shallow hold. The water did not need to be so deep. At certain times of the year the water was really too low, though, and the boats could only come as far as what was known as Cow Island. These boats did not sink too deep into the water, and all had side- or stern-wheel paddles. The decks were built high so that a lot of goods could be loaded on, as well as a lot of passengers.

The newspaper called the *Benton Record* (now the *River Press*) records the fact that the fare from St. Louis was about three hundred dollars, depending upon what kind of accommodations you had. This was for cabin passengers. Freight was brought up at the rate of twelve cents per pound. Chouteau had great faith in his boats and brought up lots of famous people. Three hundred soldiers and Major Blake came up in 1860. The two boats which carried them up to Benton were the *Chippewa* and the *Key West*.

You can still get the feeling of the old river-boat days if you stand on the bridge and watch the flow of the old Missouri. A person can picture the Indian days and the old fort, the fur traders and the soldiers guarding it.

This was a different kind of fort down here on the river from most of the others in the territory, for it was, first of all, a trading post. The measurements of the original fort are interesting to anybody today. The walls were eighteen inches thick and twelve feet high, and made of two-story proportions. The fort was 190 feet on one side and 150 on the other.

Now on the opposite corners, as I show you in the drawing, were the bastions, or lookout stations. You can see how wonderful they proved to be. Inside, too, there was a safe place for women and children to gather during Indian raids. This fort had its share of terrible stories handed down of murderous attacks on travelers near the fort and attacks on the fort itself.

Cowboys from the CK spread near Glendive, Montana. Most of them
were with Bob Kennon when he saw the "ghost light" at the Chateau
de Mores. All rode white horses except the three at the top,
who rode pintos.

Moving the bed wagons and chuck outfit for the LU near Miles City, Montana.

CHAPTER XXIII

I Meet My Future Wife

LEWISTOWN is one of Montana's most prosperous and attractive cities. It is located in the geographical center of the state and is the county seat of Fergus County. In 1885, James Fergus, a wealthy sheep man, was a delegate to the Legislative Assembly, Montana Territory, from what was then Meagher County, and he later sponsored a bill which incorporated Lewistown on May 8, 1899.

In the summer of 1879, two Frenchmen, Janeaux and Paul Morase, with fifty or more families, all half-breed Indians, came from northern Montana and entered the Judith Basin. Janeaux settled on what is now the heart of the business district of Lewistown, while his friend Paul Morase established his home on land adjoining Spring Creek.

Five years before this date, a military troop from Fort Shaw, a cavalry post located on Sun River, was sent to the Lewistown area to protect the trading interests along Spring Creek, establishing Camp Lewis in honor of Major William H. Lewis, who was in command in the summer of 1878–79. Thus the name of Lewistown. It was platted in 1882 by Dr. Leon A. Lapalme at the request of Janeaux. The main street of this town is laid out almost northeast and southwest instead of being straight with the world. Many stories have been told during the passing years as to the reason why the streets are not straight. One is that Dr. Lapalme used Janeaux's orchard fence as a guide. Anyway, the camp was mapped out much as they map out mining towns. The first schoolhouse in Lewistown was a log cabin built in 1881; a frame one was built in 1883. This small community of folks was chiefly a freighting center for cattle outfits and miners until the fall of 1903. It was connected with the railroad to Harlowton. This was known as the Old Jawbone Road. Harlow was a rancher in the Moccasin Mountains. He collected money from everyone to help build this road. Everyone was buying railroad shares, and we were all supposed to be the shareholders. Long lines of people were eager to buy shares, including us cowpokes who could rake up any money. I remember very well having put in one hundred dollars. Sam Cushman was the first railroad conductor. I remember Bill Deaton going around town telling everyone that Sam Cushman was bringing in a carload of mules on his train. This was told as a joke to get everyone excited, and all the school kids in town were there to see the mules, but when the train arrived, there were no mules.

At Harwood Lake the Shonkin Roundup Association had a large dipping vat where we dipped cattle and horses for scab. We would run the horses about thirty-five miles up off the Missouri River, using cowboys in relays along the way. At Harwood Lake we had a large corral with wings jutting out on each side. Here is where we would fan these broom-tails into the corrals for dipping. I had a terrible itch which they said was the "seven-year itch," so when we had dipped all the horses, they said, "Now it's Bob's turn," and they threw me into the dipping vat. It was quite a rough experience, I can tell you, but it sure cured that terrible itch. The outside thin layer of skin peeled completely off my body. I thought sure I was going to die, for I was plenty sore for a long time. They had another dipping vat at Chinaman's Coulee, getting water from the Teton River. Here they dipped all the horses and cattle on the north side of the Teton River.

Joe Connelley worked as a cowhand on the Shonkin outfit. He and some other cowboys had been playing poker. He got sleepy

and decided to lie down and take a nap in the bed tent. There was a bunch of shavings lying near by which someone had whittled for starting fires in the Sibley stove. Someone threw a match into these shavings. Joe rolled over in his sleep and his clothing caught fire. He came tearing out of the tent yelling: "I'm on fire! Someone help me! The Connelley family's burnin' up!"

After he had made several trips around the bed wagon, Frank Rooney finally caught him and pulled him over to the chuck wagon, where there was a barrel of water and a pail. Ice had frozen in the barrel of water, so while I broke the ice in the barrel, Frank hung onto Joe. We poured ice water all over him and he really cooled off. Poor Joe! For several days after this experience he rode standing in his stirrups.

We were not allowed to have toilets anywhere near the wagon, but had to take a walk into the sagebrush. I did this one bright sunny morning, and when I raised up, the sun shone on me, and everyone said I looked like an antelope.

"There's an antelope in camp," yelled Joe Connelley and grabbed a gun.

"Put down that gun," yelled someone. "That's no antelope. That's Bob."

I'm sure this book wouldn't be complete unless I recall some stories of Knerville, or Pumpkin Center, as it later came to be called, so named from Uncle Josh records on the early-day phonographs, those affairs with the morning-glory-shaped horn. The wax records were always carefully cared for and rolled in cotton. "Uncle Josh," as some may remember, was a hillbilly character of that day. These records were mostly talking ones, and the dialogue described all the gossip and other doings of this local country burg, "Pumpkin Center."

Knerville was started by a fellow named Hoppel in the early 1900's (1902–1903). The town was built mostly of logs cut and hauled from the near-by Highwood Mountains. The buildings were set upon large rocks without any other foundation. Hoppel was a cousin of the Stillwell brothers, livestock men of this locality. He named this place Knerville in honor of the Knerr brothers, who also had ranch interests here. It was made up of a saloon; a dance hall; a little hotel with a small dining room, operated by Mrs. Witzier, a generous-hearted and kindly soul; a blacksmith shop run by John Sanders; and a post office. Its mail came out from Fort Benton by stage up Shonkin Creek over the Shonkin Divide to Knerville. In after years John W. Woodcock was postmaster at his ranch on Upper Shonkin. Leaving Knerville on the return trip, the stage went on to another post office called Steele at the Wilson brothers' ranch. Today this ranch is only a short drive by car from the town of Geraldine.

Knerville, or Pumpkin Center, as we speak of it even today, long after all the buildings have been destroyed or moved away, was a rollicky, happy-go-lucky place. The dance hall was the main social center and attraction for many miles around. People driving horses and buggies would come from as far away as Great Falls, including those who worked at the old silver smelter.

The orchestra consisted of a violin, banjo, guitar, mandolin, steel guitar, piano, and if someone could play a harmonica, well, he also joined. These musicians, sitting on a high platform in one corner of the hall, would play all night if need be. Tommy Nelson, who did all the calling for the quadrilles, also favored the folks at these gatherings with solos and he possessed a rich tenor voice. *Meet Me in St. Louis, Good Old Summertime, Rufus Rastus Johnson Brown, Hiawather, The Bird in a Gilded Cage*, and such songs were popular at that time.

Many families brought their children, some of them mere babies. Bunks were provided for all these toddlers, one bunk built up over another. There were bunks built in all four corners of this hall, each having a ladder placed in front so the mothers could climb up and stow their youngsters for the night.

At one end of the hall they had a long table which was pushed back against the wall while the dancing was in full swing, but at midnight it was brought out on the floor, covered with a white tablecloth, then laden with all sorts of food, such as wonderful homemade bread, fine cakes, pies, cookies, doughnuts, and meat —well, there was turkey at holiday season, crisply fried chicken in summer, and other meats, such as beef, ham, and venison in season. Also jellies, fruits, and pickles. It was hard to name everything these good ranch ladies brought. Also there was worlds of coffee made in a clean new boiler, the coffee being put into a sack so there would be no dregs floating in the cups.

The boys took their girls to these dances, riding two and two in couples along the country road. My wife was a small girl then, but she can recall many of these young folks coming to the ranch home of her parents after these dances, and of her mother cooking another breakfast for them. They would play the piano and sing until they grew sleepy, then the boys would go to the bunkhouse for a snooze and the girls would still chatter and nap in the ranch house. My wife's first teacher was one of these young women, Miss Laura Benton from Great Falls, whose father was an early-day district judge.

Jack and Richard Bodkin, who were in the employ of the Great Falls Meat Company, were two other young men who always had such a fine time at these dances. As far as myself, I'd ride forty miles to get to one. Sometime after this, Richard Bodkin left for Hollywood, California, getting into the movies in the old silent days, doubling for Tom Mix and other stars.

The first time I ever saw my wife was on this same country road leading to Knerville, near the old Upper Arrow Creek schoolhouse. The roundup outfit didn't work up in that country that year because there were too many established ranches there and no longer an open range. But the roundup association used to send a bunch of us cowhands up there to work this country, all the way to Great Falls.

One time we were drifting a large herd of cattle in this section when all at once, it seemed out of nowhere, came two small girls riding a long-legged race mare as fast as she could run. Both were in a saddle with long stirrups and these were popping up and down like mad.

"Say, look how those kids can ride," said one of the boys.

One of these little girls became my wife when she grew up. I asked her years afterward why she had the stirrups so long.

"That mare wouldn't stand when you put your foot in the stirrup," she answered. "I'd put my little sister on first, put my foot in the stirrup, and pull myself up and into the saddle. If we had had short stirrups, I couldn't have reached them, and when the horse started running, I might have been dragged and my little sister thrown off. When we both got into the saddle, she could run as fast as she wanted to."

CHAPTER XXIV

A New Business

In 1902, Murphy sent me with a bunch of cattle to his Northwestern Ranch on Shonkin Creek from his Big Coulee Ranch. In the spring of 1903, I again worked as a rep at the Shonkin wagon, and that fall I again headquartered at the Northwestern Ranch. Dick Keaster and I rode all that winter gathering strays as far away as Great Falls. In 1904, I again worked at the Shonkin wagon repping for the 79, and again wintered at the Northwestern Ranch.

In 1905 the Murphy outfit, Milner's outfit, and Wearn Rowe of Fort Benton pulled out of the Shonkin Roundup Association, starting a wagon of their own. Bill Carver was supposed to be roundup foreman, but there were several other would-be bosses. Milner could see things were not running as they should, so he sent for his foreman, Jaycox, who worked for the Milner interests at Glasgow, to come up to the Shonkin country, bringing a wagon, several good cowhands, and his son, then a young boy. Everything took shape when Jaycox took over, for he was a top hand who could also handle men. He ran the wagon that year, but these three outfits only ran a wagon this one season, rejoining the Shonkin wagon the following year when Cy Buck was roundup foreman for the Shonkin outfit.

Murphy had now sold out his Northwestern ranching interests and I was no longer in his employ, but worked as a cowhand on my own, working for the Merrick Cattle Company at Geyser. I next worked for the United States Forest Service in the Highwood Mountains when the association rider quit, or until the roundup was finished. Then I worked for Patterson's near Shonkin. This was known as the Lost Lake Livestock Company, and I only worked there a very short period, going from there to Cy Buck's ranch in this same locality. We once decided to take a trip into Fort Benton in the buckboard, and while we were driving along, we saw about a dozen or more men walking around the range land in every direction. We drove over to talk with some of them. Almost in one breath they asked advice as to where they could take up a homestead. We told them anywhere as far as they could see. We drove on and the thought hit me, "Why don't we start a feed and wagon yard like they have down in Texas?"

"Let's start a feed yard in Fort Benton and be partners," I said to Cy.

"What sort of a business would this be? I've never seen one," he answered.

So I explained how it was built and managed, and he agreed we should go right on with the venture. We bought a house and four lots in Fort Benton from a fellow named Samples. We let him keep the house and he moved it off the lot. We bought the lumber from Powers, and it was hauled to the building site, where we began the building with five or six carpenters we had hired.

The homesteaders came in droves, and so needed a place to stable their teams while hauling lumber and other supplies to their claims. People flocked in here to Montana from almost every state. We had a bunkhouse and cookhouse where they could cook their own meals. We also kept three rooms in the Fort Benton hotels, one at Chouteau House, one at Grand Union Hotel, and one at the Overland, where the women and children could stay overnight when the weather was stormy and cold. We also had a secondhand store where farmers could buy and sell furniture and stoves for their homestead shacks. We bought all the old Shonkin roundup horses, broke them to work, and sold them as teams to farmers. We also had a blacksmith shop for their convenience.

Not all of the settlers were poor. Many had sold fine farms in other states to live in "The West." Many shipped in livestock, especially fine draft horses, good farm implements, and fine house furnishings as well. Others built fine two-story homes, a tribute to their belief in this raw, untamed country. Early-day people who had come to Montana as far back as the days following the Civil War settled on the rivers and large creeks, many building up fine ranches, grazing their herds of cattle and sheep up on the bench land, which grew lush grass to feed their herds. With the coming of the homesteaders, this curtailed their ranching operations because of the fencing of the free range. If they wished to continue in business, they had to operate on privately owned land. These stock ranchers controlled water rights on the rivers and creeks; thus the farmers had no water supply except from the wells they dug. These would go dry in times of prolonged drought, leaving them without a water supply for homes or livestock. Some built large dams or reservoirs, which served the purpose very well in wet, rainy seasons.

The poorest folks, bringing all their worldly possessions as well as their families, came by railroad in immigrant cars: livestock, farm implements, etc., in one end of the car, their families sharing the other end. All were eager to begin a new life here in Montana, little realizing what terrible odds they faced. The winters were long and cold, with blizzards and below-zero temperatures. Living out a winter in board shacks without an ample supply of fuel or food, or the long, hot summers with no rain except a few scattered showers, the hot sun blazing down, burning up their grain crops—all these things were not encouraging. Tractors were unheard of in those days. All farm work was done by horses, long, hard hours in the fields, riding a sulky plow. Some of the well-to-do ones had those big steam rigs, using them for breaking sod, and power with which to thresh their crops if luck held out so they had a crop. They didn't summer-fallow and so didn't have any reserve moisture in their soil. Not many planted winter wheat until some of them began to adopt this practice from their neighboring states, the Dakotas.

Doctors would be called out from Fort Benton to visit sick folks, just miles from anyplace. They would come to see me at the feed yard, saying, "Bob, will you take me out to such and such a family or location? So-and-so is sick out there. I know you know every coulee, hill, and creek in this whole expanse of country, so will you please take me out?" "Yes, I'll go with you," I would say, so they would hire a livery team and buggy, get their bag, and away we would go out into what seemed nowhere on some dark, stormy night, muffled up in beaver or racoon coats, fur caps, and mittens, to minister to these poor, lonely, sick folks. We didn't carry on much conversation as we drove those cold, lonely miles, but each had his own thoughts.

Many times the stork would have arrived before the doctor reached the home of these folks. Many had only one room in their shack, the children sleeping on the floor. The doctor would go inside while I sat outside in the buggy holding the team. Many, many times I sure had the blues just wondering what sort of evil times had come to all this vast range land I had come to know and love so well. All these doctors were good, kind Christians, enduring many hardships, often receiving not a single penny for their ministrations to the sick and dying.

One homesteader built a big two-story house on land which had been owned for years by the Kingsburys near Harwood Lake. He built the house near a smaller lake, called Kingsbury Lake, where there was a large spring of excellent water. I was riding over in that locality when I saw this new house, so I rode over to see who was living there. A big German said he had "located" there. I told him this land belonged to the Kingsburys and they had homesteaded it years before. "You folks now have a new two-story house on the 160 acres at Kingsbury Lake," I told Lew Williams, ranch manager for Kingsbury for many years. The homesteader looked this up at the land office and was advised that his claim should have been ten miles from where he located. He had to move his house down there to the right location.

Another fellow built a house on Jergen Engellant's horse pasture a half-mile from Engellant's ranch house. Another located on a school section which was owned by Oscar Johnstone. Another land locator located four different persons on this same piece of land.

A fellow who worked in the United States Land Office at Washington, D.C., wrote a letter to Judge Tatten at Fort Benton asking who this fellow Bob Kennon was, for his name had appeared as a witness for about three hundred homesteaders when they were proving up their claims. "Bob Kennon is a cowboy who knows all the land for miles around here and has a feed barn here in Fort Benton where all these settlers stay when they come into town," answered the Judge.

CHAPTER XXV

Stock Inspector

IKE ROGERS was elected sheriff of Chouteau County in 1913. I was then appointed deputy state stock inspector, a position Rogers had held until his election as sheriff. Two and a half years of my term as stock inspector were filled in Chouteau County. The other year and a half I served as stock inspector in the Big Hole country around Dillon. There were many large cattle outfits in the Big Hole, as well as smaller ones. During the time I spent as an inspector in Chouteau County, I was often deputized to act as a deputy sheriff, aiding in the arrest of lawbreakers and taking fellows who had broken the law to the state prison at Deer Lodge.

The Phillips outfit had a cattle ranch near Malta. They had an old trapper who was known to everyone around there as Tex. Tex was a wolf trapper, and a good one. Many wolves were in this section and they caused much loss to stock growers, killing steers, always picking the biggest, finest ones they could find. All the money Tex could make was from the bounty paid on the wolves he caught, and the wolf hides if he could sell them. Tex had an old log cabin down on the Missouri River. All he had around his camp was one old saddle and two of the biggest house cats I had ever seen. He was very fond of these cats, and had named them Corbett and Fitzsimmons for the two prize fighters.

Phillips seemed to have an idea that Tex was butchering his beef, so he sent for me and told me to go down to Tex's cabin and pay him a visit to see what I could find out. Now Tex was a kindly, good-natured old fellow, so when I went to see him he invited me to have dinner with him. After we had eaten, I told him of my errand.

"Yes," he said, "I'll gladly take you to the place where I have the beef hides."

We got the saddle horses and rode about two miles down on the north side of the Missouri River. We reached a spot on the river where there was a big air hole.

"Can you dive?" he asked as he looked at me. I just laughed.

"Well," he said, "that's where I threw the beef hides. I only kill what I need for myself and cats. Anyhow, I kill all the wolves which would kill Phillips' steers, so I don't think he's out very much, and shouldn't begrudge me some beef."

We rode back to Tex's camp. I spent the night there with him, for I liked the old rascal. He was so candid and truthful with his answers. When I saw Phillips, he asked me what I found out at Tex's, and I told him that Tex took me down to the river and showed me where he threw the hides.

"I think you'd better forget all about that small loss," I said, "for he does kill all the wolves, as you very well know."

He looked sheepish and answered, "Yes, I guess you're right about that."

Another time I was down on the Missouri at Virgelle, below Fort Benton. Half-breeds from the Big Sandy were butchering ranchers' stock. I would go down along the river after dark and lie in wait to see if I could catch them. I had been along the river almost all night and thought I would go home to the Blankenbaker Ranch before daylight so no one would see me. I put my saddle horse in the barn and was sure hungry. I had a room in the ranch house. Mrs. Blankenbaker always told me to go into her pantry, where I could find pies, cake, or anything else I might like for lunch, so I made for the pantry. Mrs. Blankenbaker had set a trap in the pantry to catch a pack rat. I put three fingers in the trap and sure let out some loud cussin' when I got caught. She heard me and came to the pantry from upstairs.

"Bob," she said, "did you get caught in the rat trap?"

"I sure did," I said. We couldn't keep from laughing, and she got lunch for me, after which she sat awhile and talked with me before I went to bed with my sore paw.

Another time, I met Blankenbaker in Big Sandy.

"Bob," he said, "come out to the ranch with me. I have a problem."

He had a large sheep ranch, with sheep camps scattered all over the range. He had chopped firewood and hauled it all to his sheep camps, but hard-up settlers kept stealing the wood.

"Bob," he asked, "what shall I do with these fellows anyhow?"

"Bore some holes in some of the sticks of firewood," I answered, "and fill them with dynamite, but be sure to warn all the sheepherders not to take any of these sticks of wood."

"I'm desperate," he said, "so I'll try your plan."

It wasn't long until a roof was blown off a settler's house. One told another about this, and soon the wood stealing stopped.

Mr. Lovingers had a stock ranch on the south side of the Missouri River below Billy Kingsbury's ranch. There was also a bunch of tricky breeds down there. They would come to Lovingers and ask if Bob Kennon was anywhere around. "No," Lovingers would say, "we haven't seen him for some time," and many times I would be right there on the ranch.

The badlands of Arrow Creek were a hiding place for all the cattle rustlers for miles around. I was ordered to go down there and look into some of this lawlessness. I took a saddle horse and left Fort Benton, bent on catching some of these lawbreakers. I stopped at the ranch of the Audet family, and told them my name was Jones, that I was from north of Big Sandy, and that I had lost some cattle and had trailed them for some distance down into

Arrow Creek. This ranch lady had one of my feed-yard calendars hanging on her kitchen wall. It pictured an early-day automobile stuck in the mud, hub deep, and a fellow with a big team of horses pulling it out. I laughed to myself when I looked at this calendar. She told me to go to the schoolhouse and get her son and he would take me to an old abandoned well down on Coffee Creek where they were known to throw all the hides from butchered cattle. I gave the boy a dollar and his mother didn't want him to take it. They couldn't keep me at their home overnight, so she told me to go to the home of her bachelor brother. I did this and he and I walked quite a distance back to the old abandoned well. We took a lantern and a long pole down in the well and searched for hides. I stuck my hat up on this pole and someone above shot a hole in it. The fellow in the well with me said he knew who was doing the shooting. I got some information on this shooter and caught up with him later and arrested him. He told me all about the whole dirty business, also implicated his brother and five others. One of these rustlers was a large, tall man, all of six feet, two or more inches. He seemed to be the brains of the gang, so I waited for him to come to the ranch of some of his neighbors to get his mail and arrested him. The law officers in Lewistown had told me he was really a hard character and that he had been in trouble before. He was sentenced to a seven-year prison term, but he had a wife and family who would be destitute, so he only served a part of his sentence when they paroled him so he could return home and care for his family, provided he would live as a law-abiding citizen.

Along about 1912 or 1913, Chouteau County was divided so that Hill, Blaine, and Phillips counties were created from it. There was considerable butchering northeast of Chester about this time and most of it was illegal. The deputy sheriff of Hill County, with Havre as his headquarters, was unable to locate any evidence. He notified the Livestock Board at Helena of this fact

A chuck wagon on the Musselshell. The boys are having a beef barbecue.
Bob Kennon, wearing white shirt, vest, and white hat, is sitting by the
fire next to the bearded man tending the beef.

Fort Benton, Montana, in the days before the railroads. Steamboats
brought freight up the Missouri River to Fort Benton, and bull teams
hauled it from there up the Mullan Road to Helena and
the gold camps.

and they wired me at Fort Benton to go up there and investigate. When I arrived at Chester, I was met by the stock inspector and the deputy sheriff.

It was the owner of a dry-land farm whom they had been watching, so out we drove in a spring wagon with a fast team. This place had been noticed having a lot of visitors coming and going lately, some of them known to be storekeepers and butchers. We surprised the owner just as he came out of a grainery with a quarter of veal on his shoulder. No one had noticed our approach, as it was still quite early in the day.

He claimed that it was his own calf, but when we asked to see the hide, he looked worried and acted guilty. He said his dog had dragged it off someplace, he didn't know just where. He produced the dog, a small bob-tailed animal which played about with us for a while, and I kept taking in every detail of the spread. Near by were several old barns and a big manure pile. What seemed a little out of place on this dry-land ranch were several fine saddle horses. I walked over to an old wagon box and after examining it, satisfied my mind that the stains in it were bloodstains. The dog kept showing me that he was interested in it, too, as well as in an ash pile which had been disturbed by a shovel. A trail of ashes led over to an old outhouse toilet, and I asked this fellow, who spoke with a strong Swedish accent, just why he was filling up the vault there with ashes. "My missus," he answered, "she don't like the smell, or the wind, or the flies on hot days. She's so clean and particular, you know." He laughed as though it was a joke. I felt, however, that this calf hide was there buried by the ashes in this filthy vault.

The Swede said he would have to go on with his fencing up in another pasture so if we didn't mind, he would get along on one of his saddle horses. The deputies and I decided to shovel out some of the ashes from this vault, and sure enough, there was a hide buried.

When the Swede looked back and saw what we were doing, he returned home and gave himself up, throwing himself upon our mercy. He claimed he had taken to butchering cattle because he was hard up and couldn't make a living. He led us to the manure pile, and under it were dozens of hides. We filled a couple of gunny sacks with hides for evidence and drove back to Havre to catch the train. The conductor made us leave the bags outside the cars. I was afraid they might get tossed off, after all our hard work and trouble, so I decided to stay outside the car and watch them. The deputy sheriff had this Swede in custody, and we arrived safely. The criminal pleaded guilty and Judge Tatten gave him one year in the state prison. However, we got up a petition and he was out after six months. Years later I met him at Shonkin and he said to me, "Bob, you made a man out of me, and I've gone straight ever since I got out on that petition." This thing of illegal butchering became a thing of the past in the Chester area.

It was while I was stock inspector that Judge Tatten sent me and his deputies out on a case in the foothills. This matter involved the sale of mortgaged property, and we were to arrest a man and bring him into Fort Benton. His ranch was on the east side of the Highwoods. The complaint stated that this fellow had gotten into debt with a Benton firm and then mortgaged his stock to this company. It was fine weather, and we took the Judge's team and spring wagon for the trip. This ranch joined a bachelor's whom we all knew, so when we reached there, we stayed for supper. Here we learned that our wanted man was at home on the next ranch and had been seen making hay with his sisters the day before.

We were up early the next morning, and taking my field glasses, I observed the goings on in this hayfield beyond. The two ranches were separated by a long barrier of rimrocks, which are common in this part of the mountains; they form natural fences and walls. This one was higher than a tall man and had sort of peepholes here and there in it, almost like a fort. From this vantage point we could see a group of women, dressed in light summer dresses and with sunbonnets on, making hay. One would drive along and the others would pitch forkfuls of hay up on the rack.

I watched for a while, and then I noticed something. One of these women, dressed in sunbonnet and a light-pink dress, walked over to a haycock, and sticking the fork into it, lifted the whole thing up on the high wagon rack. "Sure is a powerful woman, and handy with the fork," I said to myself.

I told the rest of the fellows to stay there while I went up the coulee to where I could come down to within fifteen feet of the haystack. The woman in the pink dress spotted me and began to run. I recognized *him* now, so I pulled down on him and commanded him to halt. He did, but begged me to let him go into the house and change his clothes. He was wearing a big, loose Mother Hubbard dress. I took no chances on his getting away from us, so I refused him. He balked like hell, but was afraid to disobey.

We ate lunch at our bachelor friend's place while the prisoner sulked in his dress, then we set out for Fort Benton. We made a quick trip coming in, you may be sure, and didn't spare the horses. Going straight to the courthouse, we noticed quite a crowd gathered about and learned there was a wedding party starting out to the church after getting a marriage license. I took my prisoner right through to the sheriff's office, and that crowd just watched, speechless, for they couldn't understand what this fellow was doing dressed up in pink gingham and hayseeds.

Neal Ballantine was a rancher who lived quite a distance out of town, and one spring he had a lot of trouble because of a fight he had with one of his hired hands. It seems that this fellow declared that Neal had shorted him on his winter wages and he wouldn't leave the ranch until he got his full amount of pay.

They got into a terrible fight, and this fellow threw Neal right through a window onto a red-hot cookstove. Then he went to Benton and reported to the sheriff about Neal shorting him on his wages. We sent word to Neal to come into Benton, but he refused to come, so I took a livery rig and went out to his ranch. When I asked him why he didn't answer the summons, he said: "Hell, I burned the seat out of my only pair of pants, and Lord, look at these blisters on my stern end!"

While I served as a state stock inspector, my services were often sought by different sheriffs to assist them in the capture of lawbreakers. The following incident is one I recall most vividly. Charlie Richards, a deputy sheriff with headquarters at Zortman, asked my help in trailing and capturing a Canadian half-breed who had escaped from Stone Mountain Prison in Canada, where he was serving a life sentence for murder. No prisoner had ever escaped from there before, for a large force of Canadian Northwest Mounted Police was stationed there. The Mounties took up his trail, but he crossed into the States near Coutts, north of Sweetgrass, and hid out on the Fort Belknap Indian Reservation, near Harlem.

The Mounties notified us and asked our help. We first struck his trail at the Coburn Ranch in the Malta area on the north side of the Missouri River. He had stopped to get some grub and feed his horse. From this ranch we trailed him to where he had crossed the river at the power plant. Now he was on the south side of the river, and we followed him on a road which led to Lewistown. Down this road a short distance, another road from Rocky Point connected with the one leading to Lewistown. Here our Indian changed the shoes on his saddle horse. He had a horseshoeing outfit and horseshoes fastened on his saddle. He turned the hind shoes backward on his horse's feet, leaving the front ones in the right position. This had Charlie and me quite puzzled at first. Soon he turned east for a few miles, going to the Marquette Ranch on the Missouri River. Marquette was a Frenchman who raised horses. We stopped and learned that our man had stopped there. During the day and night he was there, Marquette didn't realize who he was or know that he was an escaped prisoner. In those days no one asked a traveler his business. You were welcome and treated well because people lived such distances and were so isolated that often days and weeks passed without seeing anyone, especially certain times of the year.

Marquette's daughter, Ida, told us he had been there and gave us a very accurate description of this fugitive. Marquette told us that the fellow had two six-shooters, a rifle, and a fast horse. He went eight or ten miles down the river and made another stop, ate supper, and stayed all night. He molested no one and gave no hint of what he was doing, but seemed to be in a hurry. He had slept in the haystack on one of these places and was asked into the house for breakfast. He seemed unfamiliar with the country and was always asking questions. All the people knew about him was that he was a stranger.

The next time he was low on grub, he visited the ranch house of an old couple who ran a small store and post office. A big fellow who carried mail to this locality from Lewistown told us he, too, had seen him. This mail carrier, whom I have mentioned before, was called The Gallopin' Swede because he carried mail on foot, making excellent time on his route.

After making some inquiries, we followed the breed farther down to the mouth of the Musselshell River, where we stopped for the night. In our trailing of him we kept as far behind him as was safely possible, waiting for a chance to take him by surprise. He had not spotted us yet, nor had we yet come in sight of him, but we were sure by now that he was our man. His horse was now reported to be about given out. The poor animal had come much farther than our mounts had. A rancher told us that he could not be much farther ahead of us and was probably camped off the trail resting his horse.

Next morning we left at daylight and reached the next ranch early. We could see that this place had a lot of log buildings, including a long log ranch dwelling. This was quite a large ranch, raising cattle and horses, too. We hid behind some trees until we could see a light in the ranch house and smoke curling from the chimney. We knew the ranch family would now soon be having breakfast.

In those days the postmaster at some stopping place would send out mail by riders who passed, and lots of times a rancher who had not had his mail for weeks might be surprised when some rider arrived with it. Even a stranger would bring the mail to ranches he was passing as an act of kindness. Charlie said he would tell this rancher that we had the mail out on his saddle and thus conceal our real purpose and identity. This was getting too close to the criminal for comfort, and we were thinking of those two six-guns and that rifle which Marquette had warned us about.

We waited a short time before going up to the house. Luckily, no dogs were barking to announce our arrival. Soon we saw a tall man come from the barns. He was an Indian, and we could see that his height and build answered the Mounties' description to the letter. It gave a fellow a sinking feeling, but we were bent on getting him for the Mounties, and we kept thinking of that five-hundred-dollar reward, dead or alive.

We could smell coffee and bacon, and though I was sure hungry, for we had left our last stop before breakfast, we felt no real enjoyment at the prospects of eating with this criminal. At Charlie's knock, a call to come in answered us. We stepped inside the door. The family was at breakfast, and seated at the back of the table was a very tall, large, dark-complexioned fellow. The rancher sat at the head of the table and his wife at the other end, their daughter sitting opposite the Indian.

"We brought your mail out," said Charlie, and pretended to be going into his shirt for it, but instead came out with a gun and held it on the big fellow behind the table. The little girl got down in a hurry and crawled under the table. The rest of the family sat in deathlike silence for no one dared to speak.

"Put the bracelets on him, Bob," Charlie said, and I climbed over the table bench and handcuffed him, and did some disarming.

"Aren't you going to allow him to finish his breakfast?" asked the rancher's wife.

"Yes," I replied. "He can use both hands and finish his meal."

During all this time the fellow had never said a word. He finished his breakfast and Charlie ordered him to get up and come along. I went out to the barn and saddled his horse. We took his Winchester from his saddle, also a pistol from his saddle pocket, as well as a plentiful supply of ammunition. Charlie told him to mount his horse and he did so without offering any resistance. I took the lead on my horse, the half-breed next, and Charlie followed behind. We now had a twelve- or fifteen-mile ride before we would reach a ferry on the north side of the Missouri River. This was Legg's Ferry and the old ferryman took us and the horses over to the north bank, and from there we traveled toward Zortman all day.

It was growing dark when we saw a light not far away. "Let's go over there to that light, Charlie," I said. We rode to this camp, where some breeds were cutting posts and wood for the Phillips outfit. We took care of our prisoner by putting leg irons on him and chaining him to a big tree. He ate a good supper and lay down on his saddle blanket. That food was the best I had tasted in years, it seemed to me. We were very tired, too, but dared not go to sleep. Charlie dozed now and then, but I was too afraid of this criminal. Any man who was tricky enough to get away from the Mounted Police and a Canadian prison was certainly pretty dangerous.

The following morning we ate breakfast at this camp, starting out another day with our man, taking him to Landusky, in the Little Rockies, where there was an old log jail. We placed our prisoner in this jail and Charlie lighted a log fire, as the place had a damp, clammy smell. After taking off the prisoner's cuffs, we locked him safely in and went to put our horses in a livery stable before we went to a cafe to eat a long-postponed meal and bring one back for the prisoner.

As we ate and talked over our food, I felt a lot easier and relaxed after our hard trip, yet I couldn't shake off the feeling that this Indian was still with us. While we were eating, a schoolboy came in out of breath from running.

"Did you fellows put a man in jail?" he asked.

"Yes, we did," we answered.

"He'll soon be out, for he's already pried one log out," said the boy excitedly.

We raced toward the jail and sure enough, there was the prisoner with a long iron bar in his hands, standing in the corner. Charlie drew his forty-five and the prisoner raised his hands, letting the bar fall. I picked it up and removed it from the room. We then put the cuffs on him and prepared to leave for Chinook.

"Charlie," I asked, "how in hell did he get that iron?"

He explained that it must have been stuck down behind that wood stove. Of course the Indian had searched every inch of the place and had found it. A few moments more and we would have lost our prisoner.

We took him over to the cafe so he could eat. Charlie decided to leave me here and return to his headquarters at Zortman. The stage would be coming in soon, so I left my horse with Charlie, returning for him later. When the stagecoach came, the big fellow and I climbed in and went to Chinook, where I turned him over to the sheriff, wiring the Northwest Mounted Police at Stone Mountain, advising them that we had their man. They wired back, saying that I should take him on to Great Falls, where they would meet me, as they would not accept him until I took him back to the Canadian border, that is, to Coutts. Five Mounties came to Great Falls to help escort him to the border. They were equipped with everything in the way of weapons, cuffs, and leg irons. They intended to take no chances.

The Mounties and myself took him back to the border by rail. They had leg shackles connected with a long chain which they fastened to his legs. There was no way he could escape now. When they got him to the border, they took him over and I was sure happy. The Canadian government had offered five hundred dollars as a reward for his capture and return to Canada, but they didn't make good on this because we were employed by the state of Montana and were not eligible to collect this reward. However, when I retired from my job as stock inspector, I was presented with a gold star and a beautifully engraved gun with my name on the stock. I was also presented with a letter of thanks from the Royal Canadian Mounted Police for my co-operation with this force during my service at Fort Benton.

CHAPTER XXVI

Cattle Rustlers

DURING my years in the sheriff's office we had a lot of trouble with cattle rustlers and horse thieves. Chouteau County at this time was a very big county and in those days we didn't have the help in tracking down lawbreakers like they do today. We didn't have fast cars, radios, and airplanes to spot from the air into those badlands. It's a cinch now, compared to the old-time methods we were obliged to use. We didn't have tear gas, but we were good shots and had just as deadly guns.

For you to better understand our difficulties, I'd like to give you a picture of just what this country was like. There is the big Highwood Mountains section, full of caves and deep canyons and high peaks with timber which could hide a criminal. There was plenty of game upon which he could exist, and ranches at hand from which he could steal fresh horses and ride out of the country at night.

Over toward Geraldine and the Square Butte country were the lonely Missouri brakes and the badlands off toward Coffee Creek. The old Missouri River, too, could be a lot of trouble to us and certainly was on many occasions. A tracker is at a terrible loss when he comes to a river, and here the trail ends. Often a rider could completely hide his tracks for a long ways by taking the shallow water's edge and riding up- or downstream right in the river, washing out his trail behind him. He could swim his mount over and it would be hard to tell on the other side just where he crossed, too, for he could ride the shallow places here for miles in summer and fall.

The brakes along the river all look much alike, many resembling Indian tipis in shape and color. The landscape was a great help to criminals in these brakes. If you ever saw Charlie Russell's painting *Tracks Tell Tales Which Rivers Make Secret,* you will know what I mean.

The badlands in this part of the state are thick with jack pines, juniper, and sagebrush. They, like the riverbanks, were a lot of trouble to us. There is a good road through here now from Square Butte to Coffee Creek. These areas are full of ticks on the sagebrush, though no one seemed to notice these things years ago, or to give a damn about tick fever. They take tick-fever shots if they have to go over in there now. These lonely and God-forsaken places were an ideal place to run off horses or to butcher stolen cattle. They even had a place called the Hole-in-the-Wall, and no one could find out just where these cattle were brought out. There have been some terrible rock and dirt slides in here of late years, and I was unable to locate it a few years back when I had some cattle buyers from Chicago with me. We took their fast car and drove all over these roads, then got out and hiked all one afternoon, but the place had been covered.

We had to ride all over that country near Coffee Creek and Denton and even down to Winifred after stolen horses and cattle. Maybe some folks just passing through in a car and taking a tourist's view of the badlands might think them pretty, or even beautiful. I even notice some fellows are writing about this place as a perfect wonderland of scenic grandeur. To us it was just plain hell.

There are miles and miles of it, rock and slides of shale and sandstone formations. Some are giants in height, some are twisted into devils' faces and all sorts of strange critters. There is a big round rock called the Devil's Soup Bowl, and believe me, the old boy was sure there on the job cooking up trouble in it. It took tough horses and tough men, but we had both. I realized that after a hard day's riding and camping. I had passed my best days for this life, and wasn't as young as when I rode with that tough bunch of cowpunchers up the trail from the Pecos to the Powder.

Behind all these odd forms of nature we often found hides with the brands cut out, and often the whole thing carelessly dropped. It was mighty scary in there, too, and a fellow had the feeling that eyes were watching from behind those devilish forms, ready to take a shot at you. One time a horse thief from Lewistown opened fire from behind one of these places, and I guess he thought he would drive us out of there without getting the handcuffs on him. We smoked him out instead, for we had enough ammunition with us to last a week. He was sent up for a long stretch. For stock rustling there is still a stiff penalty, as strict laws were passed years ago for rustlers and they still stand on the statute books today.

Through the years we had murderers of assorted kinds. Many tragic experiences and some funny things happened too. It was all in a day's work. There was no such thing as shifts or specified hours for us. When I used to sit under the big trees in the yard of my Square Butte home, I would think of the terrible time we had with a half-breed Indian who had run there to hide from the law. He had killed a fellow up north in a drunken fight over some half-breed girl and had gotten as far as Benton. He had some friends who shielded him for days before he made his way toward Square Butte. He got away from us at Benton, but we caught him afoot near the town down here. He had guns and ammunition and was a desperate killer. We thought he would give himself up after we told him to halt, but instead he shot at us and we were obliged to take cover and try to outwit him. He made his way out of sight among the rocks and evergreen trees up on one side of the butte. His intention seemed to be to hold out until he could slip away in the darkness.

We separated and surrounded the butte. Keeping under cover in the boulder parts and sometimes crawling on hands and knees, we found a position like a sort of fort behind high rocks. As we lay in ambush I recall that there was the most beautiful pink and opal-colored sunset. That night we shot it out with him, and when he stopped firing, we knew he was out of ammunition. He wouldn't come out, so we built a roaring fire on the other side to scare him into thinking we were going to burn him out. Either he crawled into a cave for protection or was burned to death. We never knew. That fire got into the dry grass and jack pines and spread over the whole butte.

Days afterward, when things were under control and parties were organized, we covered every inch of the place but found no trace of a burned body or other evidence. We didn't go into the caves, as it was too dangerous. They were full of mountain lions. Even the criminal himself might still be in there.

This country is now cut into farms with a few hundred head of cattle where thousands once roamed on great ranches. I can see them now as we sang to the night herds to quiet them when all this was land where Milner's old J brand grazed.

Until the fall of 1883, Fort Benton was the supply base for the Northwest Mounted Police of Canada. Lawmen on both sides of the border helped one another in controlling crime, such as murder, cattle and horse stealing, and locating all kinds of wrongdoers. It is certainly a source of pride, and thankfulness, too, that for the most part these friendly relations were kept between the two countries through this medium of Fort Benton. Not only was there a lot of crime among the Indians and breeds, but the white men as well. The Canadian Pacific Railroad across the country helped considerably, but believe me, the lawmen on our side, as well as the Northwest Mounted Police, had their hands full. We helped locate "wanted" men on both sides of the border.

I look back upon the memory of these men with great respect and reverence, for they contributed so very much to the law enforcement entrusted to them. Several men lost their lives during the time we worked together, as terrible blizzards often caught them out on a patrol or on a trip to bring in some desperate character who was terrorizing some community.

Once in late October we were called up beyond the border in search of a man who was the key to a lot of extensive cattle stealing, as well as being suspected of murder. As the Canadians put it, a bad situation was fast developing between the provinces of Alberta and Saskatchewan. Many Indians and breed bands were in with the white men who carried on an extensive and illegal business. As always, these Indians and breeds were eager to carry on almost any kind of business to get guns, whiskey, and ammunition. The whole scheme had been investigated, but there were still three leaders running at large to be brought to justice. That is why we were riding north, visiting all ranches and camps and making inquiries in a roundabout way. Scarcely anyone knew us. We were trying to outmaneuver these breeds and took our orders from a sergeant of the Mounted Police. These Indians were Crees and in a strong force when they rode, as there were thousands of them in this territory.

We were well treated by all the ranchers and people whom we met, and finally found out, by guarded questions, that the leaders of these outlaws and thieves were hiding out some distance north. Because it was late in October, we were not anxious to make a long, hard trip and didn't look forward to one with favor, believe me. We were hoping to get wind of their location and return home safely to Benton before the severe cold and heavy storms set in. We joined the sergeant and his patrol riding out beyond the Cypress Hills. Some of these suspects were American citizens and some Canadian. Riding with us were men who could identify these accused fellows.

On we rode into timber and brushy country, finding as yet no clue or any trail of the wanted men. It was early evening by the time we reached our destination as directed, but the sergeant decided to wait until nightfall, so the patrol ahead was halted and we decided to make a camp well hidden from a cabin in the coulee. We were certain that we had not been sighted by anyone as yet.

This cabin was the best-hidden one I ever saw, being well down in the coulee and protected by brush and timber, but it was lonely and Godforsaken just the same. It was an ideal hide-out. Had there been snow on the ground at the time, the figures of men and horses probably would have been seen by anyone in the cabin. As I looked over this vast, rough country, I thought of what a hell of a place it would be in which to get lost. There was no settlement within miles. We made a meal of hardtack and cold tea, with some leftover beef sandwiches thrown in, and waited for darkness. Fortunately it came early at this time of year, and, too, it was suddenly growing much colder. The wind had changed to the northeast. Secretly we, too, felt lonely and I for one wished myself back home in Benton, sitting there around the potbellied stove in the office and just relating past experiences instead of living them.

We were instructed to keep quiet and warned against loud conversation. In the awful stillness even the slightest noise could be heard for some distance. As we watched, suddenly a dim light appeared in the cabin window. The sergeant took a few of us down and surprised the occupants of the cabin, finding a badly crippled white man and a half-breed Cree. They were our men, all right, and so completely taken by surprise that they gave themselves up at once. The white man's leg was painfully injured and they were short of grub. Evidently they were using this cabin only temporarily, as they had to attend to the white man's leg, which was in bad condition. You can bet he was glad to receive the excellent first aid and medical assistance from the Mounties.

That night the wind blew in a terrible blizzard and we were caught in it for a week. All hands worked next day to replenish our firewood, as we had a good fireplace here in this trapper's cabin. The wood could be dried, too, if we worked ahead of the supply. The patrol carried considerable rations of corn meal, bacon, and other staples, besides what we could get in the way of rabbits when the storm lifted somewhat.

We men from Fort Benton were depressed and worried, but the Mounties, always businesslike and trained to the hardships of this life, seemed not to notice too much. They were agreeable companions.

When the snowstorm abated, some trappers came down through this way, as this was one of their cabins. They fixed us up with some dog teams for the sick man, and the rest of us made out with our horses. The Mounties had strong, reliable animals, and as our mounts were good ones too, we finally reached Benton with our prisoner, the white man. As the Cree belonged to Canada, he was taken to one of the stations of the Mounted Police. It turned out that our prisoner was innocent of the murder charge, but was found guilty of horse and cattle theft.

CHAPTER XXVII

Some Memories

FRENCHMAN'S RIDGE is located on the old stage road out of Fort Benton as one goes to Square Butte and Lewistown. Years ago when the old fort was in operation to suppress the Indians, a Frenchman disobeyed the orders of the soldiers and went out to find an Indian who had stolen his horse and sent him in afoot. This fellow sneaked away from the fort to carry out his plan and got as far as this ridge.

Of course he was seen by the lurking Indians, who immediately killed him, taking his second horse, as well as his weapons and valuables. When his mutilated body was brought into the fort, it was recognized by one of the officers. "It's that crazy Frenchman," he declared. "He said he was going back someday to that ridge to look for his enemy." Even today this place is known as Frenchman's Ridge.

*　　　*　　　*

We old-time range men experienced a lot of bad lightning storms, and often saw stock killed before our very eyes. This kind of storm did terrible things to a herd of cattle and drove the cowboys frantic, for it often caused days and nights of extra trouble for all concerned.

However, I do remember one instance where I was obliged to see the comical side of things right in the thick of a bad lightning storm. Tom Mason and I were day-herding when a bad lightning storm came up, but Tom had always made fun of any danger and kept right on cussing and singing funny songs to the cattle. Once when a very loud clap of thunder sounded, he called out to the heavens, which were split with jagged lightning: "Come closer, Harry. Can't you do any better than that?" As he was defying the elements in this manner, a steer was struck by lightning. You should have seen him them, for his eyes almost popped out of his head. "That's all Harry! You've done enough!" he yelled.

This same summer, but somewhat later, we were night-herding for the P Lazy N and it was a terrible night. Frank Milsap was running the wagon and Healy Laird was handling the horses. I had sent a fellow in for the relief, but in this terrible storm he couldn't find me. The horses and cattle were now all mixed up and I was in the lead trying to hold them. Up under the rimrocks I could see that Healy had gotten off his horse and crawled in under the rim. He was looking out at the storm and just about terror stricken when I called out, but he was so far gone he didn't know my voice.

"Who is under that rim?" I asked.

"I'm Healy Laird, night herder for the P Lazy N," he replied, thinking he was being called by the Devil or some heavenly body.

"It's Bob Kennon, Healy," I said, "and that's a helluva place to be in."

He was greatly relieved to find that it was only me after all, and he confided later that every time he saw me spit, it looked like a ball of fire. It really was a dangerous storm, and I pulled off my spurs for fear of lightning striking the metal. I had the herd about seven miles out when the storm abated.

*   *   *

My memory often dwells upon some of the tricks we used to play on others, and one which stands out is the one we played upon a bridegroom in Benton. He was getting along in age and seemed to be afraid he would never get a wife. However, he needn't have worried so much, for an old-maid schoolteacher arrived in Benton and soon set her cap for this old bachelor.

We were all at the wedding, and after the ceremony everybody was kissing the bride and offering congratulations to the groom. We ate wedding cake, too, and by now it was getting late and the time was drawing near for the groom to take the men down to McGraw's Saloon and treat them. This groom was a tightwad, so we had McGraw loaded ahead of time to give us all the best whiskey and to get him drunk on champagne.

The saloonkeeper was with us when we went to the door and told the groom he had to go back to town and give the boys a party to celebrate his wedding. He had plenty of money, but was notoriously known as a cheapskate. He got mad as a wet hen and told us to get the hell away from there or he'd have the law on us.

While he was boiling over at the saloonkeeper, the boys hoisted me up onto the roof of the cabin and handed me wet gunny sacks which they had dipped into his rain barrel. I shoved these down the stovepipe and we got them out of the house in short order. It was cold that night, so we told him we would take the bride away to Square Butte if he didn't hurry up and come through with the money. He was too much of a tightwad to give us the party money, but said for us to go ahead and he would follow with the lady, who wished to change clothes, but we knew he was bluffing so we took her with us and he came along in a hurry.

He put a lousy five-spot on the bar and we drank it up in a hurry, the lady waiting in a near-by cafe. We told him we wouldn't let him go for her until we had our fill. It was then he began loosening up those purse strings a little.

In those days ladies were not allowed in a saloon, and far be it from any of them to even venture near the door of one. As the fun grew louder and louder, the bill for the groom grew to out-rageous proportions. McGraw made him pay every now and then, for he was afraid he might not do it later.

This was a new building which McGraw had built for his saloon and the basement had a large walk-in icehouse so that a big load of beer could be kept cold. We were pretty drunk by now and didn't care what they did to this poor bridegroom. They closed the saloon about five o'clock in the morning. The tearful bride went to Johnny McGraw's house about eight o'clock in search of the groom. She was sure she had been abandoned at the altar. He told her that the last he saw of him, Bob Kennon had him.

She came up to my room at the Grand Union Hotel, and I thought a thunderstorm was going on. She almost broke the door down and kept crying and screeching that she knew he got drunk and fell off the bridge into the river. I calmed her a little and we set out for McGraw's Saloon. He had just unlocked it, and be-lieve me, I was sobering up and becoming wide awake in a hurry.

I now remembered the icehouse. She waited upstairs while McGraw and I opened it. The groom was almost dead. We thought he was at first. Even his mustache was frozen stiff. That was the last time he ever went out with the boys, for she kept a close watch on him as long as I knew them.

*   *   *

Jack Reynolds was a bartender for Shorty Young in Havre, and as my stock-inspection work brought me up this way quite often, I got to know Jack pretty well. A lot of toughs hung around Havre, as it had everything, including honky-tonks. Jack tended bar on the night shift, and when he got off duty, he would go out in the back yard, where he had a trapeze. This setup con-sisted of two trapeze bars, below which was a deep pile of sand to lessen the fall if one should have an accident. Often they did.

Jack would perform all sorts of tricks on these bars, and said it was good exercise.

At times, when I didn't have much to do and had gotten some good tips about the characters who hung around in Havre, I would hang around with Jack, and I got to know him pretty well. After he got through turning tricks on these bars, all the drunks and gamblers would try to outdo him and each other, doing some tricks of their own. They would fall off in the sand and then get up again and hang by their knees and holler. This, of course, only happened when the weather was good, and when daylight came, they all took cover.

One morning I noticed something odd: Jack went into his room behind the saloon and got out a big sieve and took it out to the sand pile below the bars. When I followed him, he said: "Bob, you watch me and see how I make money." He then shoveled sand through the sieve until he had changed the pile entirely. During the process he panned out a lot of silver coins, and told me that some days he collected as high as twenty-five or thirty dollars.

*　　*　　*

Another thing I remember was the cattlemen's picnics in Highwood, those annual affairs which we looked forward to for months ahead, for at these we always had a wonderful time. The ladies baked beans and hams, roasted and fried chickens, made cakes, cookies, doughnuts, and homemade ice cream, and had a big barrel of lemonade. We would rather have had beer, but the wives wouldn't stand for it. We did have a lot of whiskey cached out in the pine grove, however, but this was strictly forbidden, too, and had to be consumed on the quiet as soon as we could manage it.

The ladies were always inviting us to have more and more lemonade, and we had to make a show of drinking it until they all got too busy to notice what we were doing in the pines. Maybe you don't think they were good at watching their husbands, too, and their kids driving them crazy by falling in the creek or trying to ride all the mean horses on the grounds which belonged to the younger men. Finally they would get to gossiping together and so deep in "they say" and "have you heard?" and "people say" that we practically got away with murder.

There was a fellow named Flannigan who was a perfect killer when it came to telling stories and making jokes for a crowd. He asked us to let him handle the lemonade barrel and he would get rid of it in a hurry. The ladies in charge thanked him for his kind offer with the ladle.

While I stood in front of him, he uncorked a bottle of good whiskey and began to spike the lemonade every now and then. Once he was hurrying to pick up his ladle and start to serve when an awful thing happened to him: he wore a glass eye and suddenly it fell into the barrel of lemonade.

He took out his dark glasses, put them on, and kept asking me, "My God, Bob, what shall I do? Let's dump it out."

I told him we wouldn't dare do this, as the women would never believe this unlikely story and would sure swear we were just trying to get rid of the lemonade.

"Ladle her out fast," he begged.

I told him to spike it good again to draw trade with its flavor. He would take a big swig out the bottle, too, and soon he had some real fun there with the crowd, who were by now beginning to liven up and have a fine time. He would send me for fresh lemons and sugar to kill the smell of the whiskey. Not one of the ladies had the least suspicion, and all were really drinking lemonade by the pitcherful.

It was boiling hot that day and old Flannigan would holler, "Come on up, folks, and let's give you an ice-cold drink so you can sit in the shade, drink lemonade, and kiss a fair maid." Boy, was he loaded!

Pretty soon the barrel was empty and we turned it down. Out rolled the glass eye and we lit out for the creek and washed it, then he put it back where it belonged and we joined the others. That night we played poker in the grove and I won a pile off old Flannigan. Everyone declared for years afterward that this was the best picnic the cowmen had ever held. They were loud in their praises of the wonderful lunch, and especially the lemonade.

CHAPTER XXVIII

Roped by Cupid

DURING the First World War all the young men were in army camps or embarking overseas to aid in the war against Germany. People made money in those days, grain bringing good prices, while beef, mutton, and wool were all in strong demand. They were buying cars until every family had one, mostly Fords among the ranchers—touring cars with side curtains which one must take off and put on according to the weather. Most of the ranch families, when driving, were getting stuck in the mud and having to be pulled out by teams.

We fellows with the feed yards could see that the days of horses, buckboards, and buggies were about over, so we sold out our feed barn in 1917. When I completed my last term as state stock inspector, I returned to Fort Benton from the Big Hole country. Scott Leavitt, who was then a federal forest supervisor, asked me if I would like to work for the United States Forest Service as boss in the Lewis and Clark National Forest in the Highwood Mountains. As the work entailed the handling of cattle and sheep, the attraction of an outdoor life pleased me, and I accepted the job.

I was glad to be back in the mountains working on the range again. The years I spent in the forest reserve were for the most part carefree and happy ones, as the old cattlemen were good, fair-minded fellows who knew and valued the services of an honest and loyal boss. But this was not so in later years when their sons took over the ranches to replace their dads, who had either retired or crossed over the Great Divide. I also made fine, lasting friendships while I worked on the reserve, among people from Great Falls and surrounding towns who came fishing and camping in the Highwood Mountains.

In the winter of 1923, I worked as a doorkeeper in the state senate at the capitol building in Helena. This was a very pleasant job and here, too, I made many worth-while friends. In 1924, I married the girl of whom I have spoken before. The little girl with the gray race mare was now a young lady spending the summers of 1922 and 1923 at the summer home of Sam Stephenson of Great Falls, where she and the two teen-age sons of the Stephensons spent the summer each year.

You have probably been wondering why I didn't put my brand on some female during all this time, but after I saw just what happened to a fellow's freedom when he got hitched, I fought off committing any such rash act. All of us cowboys liked to roam, and I did plenty of it. You can't do much roaming in double harness and I had never been broken to travel that way. I did most of my traveling in a lope, but taking my time where I pleased, loitering where I found good cowmen and good range. I never saw a woman that I would let take away this wonderful freedom until I started to pile up a few years, and then it was that I met Marie Boyd, my wife.

Most men, I think, always have a sort of ideal woman in their minds, and I had my ideal, too, though I never bothered to explain to anyone why I preferred her. She just had to be a small woman, and I never could stand the looks of a great big gal. She had to have dark eyes and dark hair, to be a good cook and a clean housekeeper. Besides this, she would have to like my sort of life, to be interested in ranch life, horses, cattle, and the outdoors. She would have to put up with me and my ornery ways, but I would love her and give her everything I owned. I hoped, too, that she would think the world of me in return. I had seen an awful lot of

sadness, too, with married couples, and believe me, this dis-
couraged a lot of us bachelors from taking the fatal step into
matrimony.

Lots of fellows started out with what they thought to be a
winning hand, but it sure turned out to be a losing one instead.
This was their ruin, too, for they generally turned to heavy
drinking and went to the dogs in general. They had been first-
rate fellows, too, before these mistakes had been made in choos-
ing a life's partner. I've seen men, too, who had married some
pretty little girl and then as soon as the kids came along and he
had to settle down and become a father and earn a decent living,
he would throw up the whole deal and hit the trail between sundown and the next dawn. The kids, Lord help them, suffered.
The young mother generally had to go to work in some hash
house, or worse, and before long she would generally marry
some other no-account roamer and the kids would have a stepdad
who didn't want them in the first place and would act just as
ornery as he could until he would get rid of them to some kin-
folks or strangers.

As most fellows of my day did, I knew all sorts of women.
Some would make a play for your money, some would like to
corner you and make a Christian of a wild cowboy just to say they
had reformed a man, and some simply came out from the big
cities to get a husband, no matter if he was deaf, dumb, blind,
and all these put together.

Cupid, though, is always on the job and gets most fellows
sooner or later. He had been watching his chances to throw his
rope on me for a long time, and believe me, he sure did me a
good turn, for Marie more than lived up to my expectations as to
the ideal woman I long had in mind. She was small, and
had soft brown eyes and black hair, and was altogether a very
sweet little woman.

I met her one day while she was out trail-riding with the two

Stephenson boys in Highwood Valley. She was a sort of companion, range boss, and cook for these two boys at their summer home. Their father was then president of the First National Bank of Great Falls, but he liked to keep his boys out in the country to learn something of ranch life and stock raising. He feared they might take to cement instead of grass and he wanted them to be stockmen. All during his own youth he had wanted to be a rancher, but fate seemed to steer him to be a successful man of the financial world. His boys were chips off the old block, for success crowned all their efforts. They took up the practice of law and are very successful in this field today.

They were two dandy fellows and I liked them for themselves. They were as smart as a whip and took to riding and stock just fine. Their dad used to consult me about all his stock problems, and as I was handling the grazing end of the forestry work, I was living at the ranger station there on Upper Highwood Creek.

Naturally I met Marie and these trail riders quite often, and one day when her horse went lame, I offered her my top horse from the corral at the station. About now I should have been watching out for Mr. Cupid, but you see, that's how he works. He just creeps up on the blind side of a fellow and before he knows what is happening, he is roped, throwed, and branded.

I figured that I would get real chummy with these two boys, Jack and Junior Stephenson, so I would get invited down to one of Marie's chicken suppers some night. I hoped she would have pity on a poor bachelor living there at the ranger station and doing his own cooking. Well, this scheme worked just fine. Before long, I was a frequent visitor at the big cabin, and one rainy night when we were sitting there together by the fireplace, I asked her to be my wife. Though she was generally in favor of the idea, she had, like most women, a hundred excuses and reasons for delaying the big date.

Marie was a devout Catholic and would not hear of any marriage outside the Church. It must not be a parson or justice of the peace, but a priest, who would perform the ceremony. Neither of us wished a big, fancy Wedding Mass, for one of those kind of Masses lasts all morning, it seemed to me. I had in time past been present at some of these, and I made up my mind I wasn't going to be up in front of an audience any longer than I had to. I figured to put my brand on this little filly as quick as possible.

Of course I had to go through a lot of red tape to prove that I had been baptized a Catholic by a padre back in Texas, and this took quite a long time, believe me. At last I was accepted on this score, and about a year from the time I met Marie, we were married there in Great Falls at the parish house by the Reverend Father McHough with only four relatives and close friends as guests.

"Father," I said, "this is the first experience with marriage for me and I feel jittery."

"I feel the same way," he answered, "for this is my first time to perform a ceremony." He had a keen sense of humor.

We got a big, rousing reception when we went out to Belt afterward to her mother's place, and there we had a big feed and a small wedding cake and all the fun that goes with a wedding dinner. Then, as was the custom, the kids of the town all came and put on a show, with tin cans rattling and cowbells ringing. Then, as was also the custom, the bride and groom came out and the groom showered down handfuls of coins. We did all this and enjoyed every minute of it. We had open house and all the townsfolk came and wished us well as we left for our honeymoon in Yellowstone National Park.

It is a funny thing to me, and sort of sad, too, how things change, for we went back there some years later and the whole thing seemed to be much less attractive than it had been before. It seemed to me that the geysers were less thrilling, the mountains only half as high, the canyons not nearly as wide. Maybe it is because on a honeymoon a man sees everything about him through a mist, and everything, even the most commonplace, seems beautiful. That is how it was with Marie and me. Though we were naturally anxious to return to our ranching interests, we felt a certain sadness as we left this natural paradise.

We spent the winter of 1924–25 at Helena, where I was employed again as doorkeeper for the state senate. We spent the next two years on Highwood Creek, living at the camp in summer and in town during the winter. In the meantime, we had been buying cattle, which we put out to pasture in summer and put them with some rancher in winter for winter feeding. We agreed we should have a ranch. We leased a high mountain range suitable for the cattle business on Upper Shonkin from my friend of long years, Joe Wright, and got an excellent bunch of Hereford heifers from him, running them on a share basis. Thus we acquired an excellent herd.

We made this place our home for the next sixteen years, working hard, but also having fun, for we always had a houseful of company, mostly young folks. Then Mr. Wright passed away and his nieces and nephews wished to settle his estate, so they sold all the land and the fine herd of cattle which their uncle had built into a very worth-while outfit. This ranch where we made our home was very poor hay land, so we did not care to buy it from the estate. During the years we lived there, we weathered the depression of the thirties, keeping our cattle, and I held onto my job in the forest reserve, but we did not make any progress from a financial angle.

CHAPTER XXIX

Rodeos

IN 1928 AND 1929, I tried my hand at the rodeo game by furnishing parade property for the Great Falls Chamber of Commerce. In 1928 all I had in the parade was my string of pack mules. These mules would always let out a loud bray if we were on parade at or near noon, causing much amusement among the spectators on the street. I rode a saddle horse and led the mules, six in number, all chained one to the other in a long line. The smallest had a coffee pot around his neck.

In 1929, I still had these mules and had added two stage-coaches, one an old Deadwood stagecoach, the other the famous old Red Bird, which had traveled the old stage route for years between Landusky and Chinook. Louie Goslin was the owner and operator of this stage line for years. When the stage route was discontinued, he stored old Red Bird carefully away in a dry, roofed barn at his ranch in the Little Rockies, for Louie had a real and deep affection for this old vehicle. I have known Louie for years and he later gave the coach to me as a gift and I have always prized it highly. Today this Red Bird coach is a part of the Western Collection at Old Town in Great Falls.

Then we had a covered wagon drawn by oxen which Bill Lee of Highwood had broken to work with an ox yoke. A Red River cart drawn by oxen broken to yoke was also added. These Red River carts were used by Indians in the early days. They are high, two-wheeled carts, having a railing around the body and a canvas top to keep out the cold and rain. Jack Lee gave me this cart which he had used when he carried mail from Fort Benton to Fort MacLeod. Jack trailed this cart behind his mail rig, using the cart to hold baggage, long before the days of the railroad. The ox yokes were a discovery of my own from the basement of Davis Brothers Store in Fort Benton. Today these same ox yokes are in the entranceway to the Cowboys' Museum in Great Falls.

The brick building where I found the ox yokes had been built in the early days by the Murphy-Neal Company, Ltd., and this company freighted supplies from Fort Benton, then the head of navigation. All supplies were shipped from St. Louis on steamboats, then overland by ox teams from Fort Benton to Helena on the old freight route up the Sun River Valley. All the work stock was held in a large stockade and corral where the Fort Benton school now stands. Jim McDonald was one of the early-day bullwhackers, Dick Mee another, and Robert Ford of the Montana banking family also had a freighting business.

Another trading and freighting firm was I. G. Baker Company. They had a trading post in early-day Fort Benton. Michael Byrne, a lifetime friend of my wife's family, was an accountant for this firm for years after his discharge from the Seventh Cavalry at the fort.

The old Shonkin mess wagon was also in our parade, with its original mess box and a coffee grinder with its large wheel. This was placed solidly on one side of the mess box; also a mirror was placed on one side of the wagon, for a few hands liked to shave occasionally and needed a mirror. Many early-day brands were burned into the wood of the sideboards of the old wagon box, and it had a high seat for the driver.

Grey Scott and my horse-loving friend McLain, who owned a beautiful horse ranch in the Mission range of mountains in western Montana, were partners. These two showmen furnished the horses and Indians in the parade. There were many very beautiful palominos and pintos, all fancifully decorated and ridden by the Indians, and also travois, pulled by horses, upon which squaws and papooses would ride. Should you not know what I mean by a travois, I'll try to explain. There are two poles, much like the shafts on a racing sulky. The horse wears a harness made from buffalo hides; straps made from hide go over the horse's withers and tie in a hard knot under his belly as a means of pulling the travois. The seat upon which the Indians ride is of buffalo hide, and their belongings are attached to the long poles with buffalo-hide thongs. The seat, also of buffalo hide, is not stretched too tightly, allowing it to sag some so that the papoose can ride with no danger of its falling out, or if there are many articles, they, too, will stay on safely. These Indians were from Arlee, in western Montana, and all good friends of mine. Anytime they came to Great Falls, they would always look me up and invite me to their tipis.

Another attraction at the rodeo was a clown called Overland Red, who owned one of the prettiest and smartest little mules I've ever seen. Red was sure a character, and his mule could do all sorts of tricks. He could stand on his head, sit up, play dead, and a lot of other tricks. Another funny clown was Tex Clark, who lived at Wolf Creek on his ranch. He had an old white mare which sure knew her tricks. Tex was a daredevil, for he would tease those Brahma bulls the bull riders were riding, dashing up to these ugly creatures, then back into his barrel.

I cannot forget Jack Goldberg, who makes Great Falls his home. Jack was a stunt artist with a rope, spinning as many as eight ropes at the same time. He was also a trick rider and competed with the top stunt artists of the rodeo world. He could twirl two old frontier forty-five caliber pistols with a skill which was nothing short of magic.

The Blackfoot Indian band from Browning always put in their appearance at these rodeos. They were very fine musicians, all happy and enjoying themselves playing for the rodeo crowd

and taking part in the parade. These band members had striking-
ly beautiful uniforms of buckskin, handsomely beaded and with
very colorful headdress. One Indian lady who came every year
and whom I will always remember was Mrs. Morning Gun, on
whose property oil has been discovered. The Indians' pastime
was playing that guessing game where they hold pebbles or some
object in their hand while others guess which hand holds the
object. In the evenings after rodeo hours, when all the rodeo
stock was cared for, I would go over to their camp and play this
game with them. I still enjoy taking trips to Browning, visiting
the Indian Museum and seeing my friends there.

The Reed brothers of Stanford put on all these rodeos. Mike
and Fred Reed had one horse in their large string of buckers
which no rider had been able to top. This horse was named "Who
Cares." A rodeo rider—a bronc rider from Midland, Texas—
was very anxious to ride this horse, but he had no money with
which to pay his entrance fee. He was a large, fine-looking fellow and was walking around over by the bucking chutes wearing
a long face. I was over at the chutes when I noticed him.

"What's eatin' on you?" I asked him.

"I want to see if I can draw that bronc they call 'Who Cares,' "
he answered. "I believe I could ride him, but I'm broke."

"Where're you from?" I asked him.

"Midland, Texas," he answered.

"We are two native sons," I told him. "I, too, am a Texan
from near Dallas—Cedar Hill, to be exact."

"Oh," he said, "I've been there many times."

"So you would like to get aboard 'Who Cares,' " I said.

"I sure would, pardner."

"I'll give you the entrance fee," I said. "You go see if you can
draw this killer outlaw."

"Okay," he said, "and thanks. I'll see you again." And off he
went.

Luck held for this Texan and he did draw "Who Cares." He sure was a happy cowboy now, and he really rode that horse. He sat up there scratching that old gelding front and back as far as his legs would reach, but that old bronc sure could buck. He knew every trick a horse could know, but this rider gave a genuine exhibition ride. The stands went wild. Old "Who Cares" bucked over to the gate when the whistle blew, but this fellow didn't seem to be in a hurry to quit. He just seemed to love to set this horse, probably admired him for his fighting heart and bucking qualities. Mike Reed didn't quite approve of this turn of affairs, for he said: "I'll bet old 'Who Cares' won't ever buck again."

During the depression years there arose a lot of quibbling, quarreling, and dissension among the members of the Stock Association. This was a small association composed mostly of little ranchers running a small number of cattle on forest-reserve pasture. In fact, it was a neighborhood affair bent on grazing off every blade of grass on the forest range. To this I put in strong objections, for I believed in the conservation of grass on range land. The early-day cattlemen had taught me from boyhood that the range grass was the cowman's heritage, not only for the present generation but for those who were to follow. The majority of the members disagreed with me, so I was relieved of my job, but I still knew I was holding up for what was just and fair to others.

Then I worked only for the U.S. Forest Service under Forest Ranger Stacy Eckert, who is now retired and lives in Lewistown. The district supervisor was W. W. Willy, whose headquarters were at Missoula, Montana. Both these men were princes to work with, and I again found my new work very interesting and with excellent pay. I supervised a CCC camp on King's Hill where unemployed young men, idle in depression days, could work building bridges, tourists camps, or surveying roads. These camps kept the boys busy and also taught them constructive forms of work and gave valuable training for the war years which followed. The government provided food, clothing, and shelter for these boys, many of whom were from Eastern states. Some of the boys in our outfit were from Brooklyn and the Bronx. Life here was very new and different for them, but they easily adjusted themselves, as is always the way with youth. I remember one boy we had for a cook in the Highwood CCC Camp. He was a real good cook and made fine homemade bread, cake, and pies, as well as excellent beef roasts, and his kitchen tables and the floors were marvels of scrubbed cleanliness.

We did survey work on King's Road in Cascade County; also tore down an old telephone line from Utica, Charlie Russell's old stomping grounds, to King's Hill. I did tandem work with my mules, packing long telephone poles and timber for construction work on high mountainsides where they couldn't use trucks. In this work you use one mule in the lead, the other behind, according to the length of the particular object you are packing. The timbers were lashed to the mules' pack saddles, making sure they were tightly cinched. You lashed the timbers to your lead mule, a timber to the right and left sides, until both were securely tied. Then you went through the same procedure with the rear mule. The timbers rode well in this manner, but one must judge the distance for turns and such, going up and down mountainsides. I would lead the lead mule while riding a saddle horse. All this work was done in the Little Belt Mountains. Today there is a scenic highway over King's Hill, which is above the old silver-mining towns of Neihart and Barker. In Monarch Canyon on King's Hill there was the largest collection of arrowheads I had ever seen anywhere in Montana. Collectors of arrowheads found many varied and beautiful heads here.

In later years Mr. Sam C. Ford, governor of Montana, appointed me to the job of guard at the state liquor warehouse at Helena. I held this job during all of Governor Ford's administration and part of Governor John W. Bonner's, the succeeding governor, in all, about ten years.

In 1942 we bought a small stock and wheat ranch in the Sun River country. This ranch is on the north side of Sun River a few miles above old Fort Shaw. We ran our cattle there and had a ranch couple run sheep on shares.

In the meantime my wife found an abandoned gray granite house in the old cow town of Square Butte. She told me she would like to buy this beautiful old house, and I having no objection, she bought it and we found that it was not too badly in need of repair. We hired a carpenter and he repaired and rewired the house, turning it into a charming, attractive home. We left the ranch and lived in this house from 1950 to the spring of 1953, when we returned to the ranch, making it our permanent home. In 1949 we had sold the cattle, for we had now discovered this to be ideal sheep country, and not adapted to cattle raising, being too cold in winter. It was short-grass country, although there is an abundance of bluejoint grass too.

When my sister, Mrs. Addie Roberts of Dallas, Texas, paid us a visit, she tried very hard to induce me to sell out and return to Texas to live out the rest of my days. "Once a Texan, always a Texan," she said, "and you must be laid to rest in Texas soil." I disagreed with this plan and told her I didn't claim Texas any more. I belonged to Montana, where I had spent all my adult life. Addie was disappointed in me and cut her visit short, returning to Dallas. We invited her to visit Yellowstone and Glacier parks while on her visit, but she declined, saying she just couldn't understand her brother Bob's refusal to return home.

The house in Square Butte remained closed and in the custody of a caretaker. The wheat farming here on the ranch was taken care of by a very able farmer, Claude Welsh, who lived in the near-by town of Simms. We ran a flock of sheep here on the ranch, buying our foundation stock from the Hughes Livestock Company of Stanford, breeders of excellent sheep. We take care of these sheep ourselves except the shearing and the docking of lambs. We now have a nice flock of Columbia and Rambouillet cross, all open-faced sheep producing for the most part fine and halfblood wool. We have tried retired living in town, but found we were lonely and unhappy, not having any constructive work or business interests to take up our idle time. We moved back to the ranch and now live a very enterprising, busy existence, finding new interests as the months pass.

Our ranch is located on what was once the boundary line of the Blackfoot Indian Reservation, and a large creek called Blackfoot Coulee Creek flows all the way across this ranch. In the early days this was all Indian country, with a government Indian school operating at Fort Shaw. It is for the most part filled with valleys and hills, with a wide expanse of bright blue sky overhead dotted with beautiful white cloud formations. We take outdoor pictures, and the sky and clouds are always the most outstanding features of the pictures. There are many purple buttes, like those in the paintings of Charlie Russell. One has only to walk up on a hill above the ranch house to view the glorious sunset, when it dips behind the majestic Rocky Mountains.

We have a large ranch yard with beautiful old shade trees planted many years ago by the first settler on this land, also shelter belts and hedges and evergreen trees which our niece, Peggy, and I have planted. There is always a large vegetable garden, but most of the large amount of vegetables go to our friends, as I raise this garden for the sheer joy of doing so. There is also a strawberry bed and a flower garden, and we have sheep dogs, chickens, saddle horses, work teams, and a pet Manx, that tailless breed of cat. Our home is one of those old two-story ranch houses built in the early days with plenty of room for fun, and here we entertain our friends, for we have always had what one would call "open house" since we were married. Among our relatives there are several couples having small children which we love dearly and enjoy having them visit us.

One fall a few years ago, my nephew and his wife came to visit us, driving up from their home in Dallas. I had last seen him forty-five years before when he was just married. We live along a highway, and one day I saw a car stop at the gate. The occupants just sat there, and I told my wife I had better go out and see what they wanted. I went out to the gate and greeted them.

"Good morning," I said.

"Good morning," they answered.

Then my nephew, Bill, asked if a fellow by the name of Jones lived there and said he had heard a man by that name had some sheep for sale. I told him no Jones lived here and there was no rancher by the name of Jones anywhere near here.

"Well," he said, "would you sell me some of those sheep?"

"Those sheep are not for sale," I answered.

Then he opened the door of the car and stepped out. He asked me to let him read the palm of my hand.

"You came from a large family, didn't you?" he asked.

By this time I didn't know just how to take him. "How in hell do you know anything about my family?" I asked.

"Uncle Bob, don't you know me?" he asked, laughing.

"I sure don't," I answered.

"Why, I'm your nephew Bill Treese from Dallas. We have come to take you home to Texas," he answered.

I asked them in, and by this time my wife was out at the gate, too, so they drove their car in and came into the house. They would only stay two days and said they must get back to Dallas before a snowstorm hit up north. He kept begging me to sell out and live out the rest of my life in Texas, but I refused.

CHAPTER XXX

Around Helena

BACK IN 1950, Marie and I went over and joined in the centennial celebration of the founding of Fort Owen, on the site of old St. Mary's Mission. The mission itself was established in 1841 by three Jesuit priests, Father Nicholas Point, Father Pierre Jean De Smet, and Father Gregory Mengarini. In 1850 the mission was sold to Major John Owen, who was a good friend of the Flathead Indians and handled things there for the government for many years. Thus the fort took his name.

A lot could be written about the Flathead Indians, but I think perhaps the most interesting thing is the fact that one of the men raising the flag on Mount Suribachi in the picture which has become so famous is Charlot, grandson of Chief Charlot. The first Charlot was chief of the Flatheads. He was tricked by white men into leaving his beloved home in the Bitterroot Valley to go to a reservation called Jocko. His father had been Victor, who fought so hard to keep the Bitterroot for his people. Young Charlot was killed on Iwo Jima and the Indians were very proud of him, and indeed they should be, for he had proved himself to be a great warrior like his ancestors.

For years when I was doing brand inspection I spent a few months off and on at the ranches in the Bitterroot Valley. It always was a fine valley for stock raising, especially horses. I bought several fine saddle horses from this section. Marcus Daly was one of the famous copper kings of Montana who raised horses at Riverside and founded the Bitterroot Stock Farm. I would like to mention that one of Daly's most famous horses was the thoroughbred he called Tammy. This horse's likeness is done in the inlaid hardwood floor of the dining room of the Montana Hotel at Anaconda, Montana.

Another of his fast race horses was a horse called Ogden, which was the grandsire of Zev, the winner of the Kentucky Derby in 1923. Daly himself died in 1900. This same year, his horses ran first, second, and third in the American Futurity. A year or so later, all these beautiful horses were sold in Madison Square Garden.

This great estate which was built here in the valley was called Riverside. It was a dream place, and if you look in the stalls of the grand stables, a real horse lover can almost see and hear those beautiful horses. The fields of green lay idle where these beauties once frolicked and pranced in gay high spirits. I liked to come here, as these were wonderful people.

Every time I go to the Capitol, I always remember my years there at the Senate. And I always make a short pilgrimage to the chamber of the House of Representatives. There is the great painting I always love to look at, done years ago by Charlie Russell. It is on the wall behind the speaker's desk, and the figures of the men and horses are nearly lifelike. It shows Lewis and Clark meeting with the Flathead Indians at Ross's Hole near the Idaho border. Many consider this his masterpiece, but you've got me when it comes to that, for all his paintings seem like masterpieces to me. This one is tops, though, as any old range man and cowpuncher can swear to its reality. The horses, the men, the grass, and all are just perfect. You can tell tomorrow's weather by his sunsets and skies. The Indians are trading furs and other things in this picture. Even the motion of the horses is there as they graze, and these horses are so real a fellow could just walk out and catch up their reins. Even those who have never ridden the range, nor a good horse along the trails, will

237

love this picture and remember it. You have to see it, for there are no words of mine or anyone's that could describe it justly. It is true to the locality and I've seen these sunsets on the range thousands of times near Square Butte and Highwood and along the Milk and Marias rivers.

This capitol building is just full of things you would love to see. If you go out on the portico and look across to the Scratch Gravel Hills, you can see a beautiful piece of nature's own handiwork, a portrait of an Indian sleeping. It is known as the Sleeping Giant. Charlie Russell used to say he felt like a poor imitation of the real thing when he looked at what old Ma Nature turned out. But Charlie was no slouch when it came to modeling and doing sculpture. The world knows this well.

Sleeping Giant Mountain is really quite a distance away, and you can see his long nose and mouth as he lies there on his back. You can see him better if you go to Klick's Camp there in the Sun River Canyon. But Charlie used to say the best Indian in Montana is near the town of Augusta. It is really a wonderful Indian face, with feathers down the back of his head like a war bonnet. Lewis and Clark called this old boy Shishequaw. When we were riding in the old days along the Teton River, we went off in this part of the country and camped several days looking for strays.

When you look at this face, it seems to be a real Indian with real Indian features. This landmark is visible from a long distance. It is the way the rocks on its southerly side are piled that creates this seemingly carved face. The gangs of stage robbers, of course, must have known every inch of the place and made it their headquarters for hiding their plunder. Here on this tributary of the Sun River was a good place to camp. There are even log cabins here and there which these robbers lived in most of the time. They were always armed to the teeth and separated so as not to cause suspicion. A lot of those fellows were even sheriffs in the daytime in Helena and near by. Some had respectable jobs and businesses of their own in working hours.

They managed this perfectly for a long time. They would mask and change horses in order to hold up a stage or a freight outfit for its gold dust and money. When a posse or band of vigilantes chased them, they often took to the hills up here near the old Chief Mountain and made extensive caches until they dared return to divide the spoils. There are a lot of interesting stories told about this mountain because the Plummer gang is supposed to have cached a lot of their loot in these foothills. You could get the creeps here on a moonlight night when someone, like the cowpunchers who used to ride here, would tell a ghost story of the Plummers coming back for their loot. They held up the freighters who came up from Fort Benton on the Mullan Wagon Road through the canyons near Wolf Creek and Helena, and the gold shipments that went out on the stages too.

The Piegan Indians kept this place sacred, and maybe it's a Piegan face we can see as we look at this piece of nature's sculpture. He sure is a mean-looking old cuss when the light shines on him just right.

It was in the 1860's during the Civil War when the famous Henry Plummer gang carried on their operations in this region, and escaped into the foothills near this mountain on the north side of the Dearborn, close to the present town of Augusta. Plummer was married to the daughter of a respectable family, and this record may be found in Helena in the Catholic Bishop's records. The ceremony was performed in St. Peter's Mission, near Cascade, at the home of a priest, Father Iomada. Plummer began his career here as a badman while also serving as a sheriff of Alder Gulch, and was unsuspected by anyone for some time.

One of the gang was captured by the vigilantes and was to be hanged. A man was always allowed to say anything in the way of a message before he swung, so this fellow dictated a letter to a bystander, who promised to send it to the unfortunate man's wife in St. Louis. In it was the information that he had left her the sum of something like thirty thousand dollars and other valuables taken in loot from the stages on the Mullan Wagon Road between Helena and Fort Benton. This letter gave directions.

The wife of this man did come and, with her son, dug for one whole summer all around this area and tore up the cabin log by log, but found nothing. They went back to Missouri and came again the next year, then disappeared. No one knows if they found the money or not. Many parties hunted treasure here in the earlier days, and many sheepherders on the ranch owned by the late Carmichael, upon whose land this mountain stands, would put in endless hours, while herding their bands of sheep, making monument landmarks and maps of the place. I think they took the herding jobs out here just to have the opportunity of doing a little prospecting for what they hoped would be easy gold.

This is a large area, and it would be hopeless to try to cover it without a professional at the head of an expedition, such as go on those long trips to Egypt to dig up old kings' tombs. It has so many rocky slopes that a fellow couldn't blast, for he would cover up too much in the fall of rocks.

Some cattlemen from Helena once went to Chicago with some cattle and while there went to a fortuneteller and asked her if she knew of any gold there. Of course she said "yes" and told them to get a thing called a "treasure finder" at a dealer's there and hunt for this metal with this gadget. They followed her advice and bought a "doodlebug," but failed to find any money.

Whenever we old-timers get together, we talk over these things. Our new and younger friends want to hear about them too. But always we speak of Charlie Russell, and each year there are fewer and fewer who knew and remember this great man, the artist and the cowboy, for Charlie was all these.

We owe Charlie Russell a debt which can never be paid, for he put down on canvas his pictures of our life as cowmen in that far-gone time when the horse was king and nature held forth her very best for us to enjoy. Where now are the great buffalo herds which came to drink? Where, too, are the longhorn cattle? The trail herds of that long ago day? Only in memories such as I recall and in the paintings of Charlie will they be found.

As I look back and remember what a lot of living I have done, there is one adventure which stands out beyond all others. Yes, you've guessed it: it was bringing that trail herd up from the Pecos to the Powder.